Dreams unto Holiness

Books by Marsha Sinetar

Ordinary People as Monks & Mystics, Revised (2007)
Don't Call Me Old, I'm Just Awakening
Sometimes, Enough is Enough
Spiritual Intelligence
The Mentor's Spirit
Holy Work
Reel Power
To Build the Life You Want, Create the Work You Love
Developing a 21st-Century Mind
Living Happily Ever After
A Way Without Words
Elegant Choices, Healing Choices
Do What You Love, The Money Will Follow
Ordinary People as Monks & Mystics (1985)

Gift & Children's (Illustrated) Books

Why Can't Grown Ups Believe in Angels?
Self-Esteem is Just an Idea We Have About Ourselves
A Person is Many Wonderful, Strange Things

Publications from T h e C e n t e r***

Can You Simply Trust?
Posture of Heart, Series, *1*
Posture of Heart II (The Mary Pattern)
Dreams unto Holiness (Inquiry Series, #1)
Posture of Heart, III (Practice: Inclining the Ear)
Posture of Heart, IV (Contemplative Study)
Posture of Heart V (Our Living Framework)

*** Center publications are limited R & D works, which, until distributed more broadly, are only available on a limited basis, until sold out from The Center, www.marshasinetar.com.

Dreams unto Holiness

Exploring the Power of a Sweet, Transcendent Sleep

Marsha Sinetar

1. Dreams— Spiritual 2. Holiness—Dreams 3.Dream Analysis —Religious; Spiritual

ISBN: 1535544104
ISBN 13: 9781535544108
1 2 3 4 5 6 7 8 9 10

For three dear friends with whom, for so many years, I have been able to discuss all things under the sun, even the spiritual side of my own dreams. I dedicate this book to Ilona Burdette, to Patty Murphy, and to Sister Florence Vales, OSC.

Table of Contents

Preview · xi

Part I · 1
Chapter 1   Our *True* Learning · · · · · · · · · · · · · · · · 3
Chapter 2   "Awakening" in Sleep · · · · · · · · · · · · · 15
Chapter 3   Transcendent Dreams · · · · · · · · · · · · · · 31
Chapter 4   Our Ongoing Framework · · · · · · · · · · · · 39

Part II · 53
Chapter 5   God & Psyche · · · · · · · · · · · · · · · · · 55
Chapter 6   The Meaning is the Message · · · · · · · · · · 66
Chapter 7   Words, Symbols, Samples · · · · · · · · · · · 80
Chapter 8   As in Heaven, So in Earth · · · · · · · · · · · 98
Chapter 9   When Stones Sparkle · · · · · · · · · · · · 108

Author's Thank You · · · · · · · · · · · · · · · · · 131
About the Author · · · · · · · · · · · · · · · · · 131

And [Jacob] lighted upon a certain place, and tarried
there all night, because the sun was set; and he took
of the stones of that place, and put them for his pil-
lows, and lay down in that place to sleep.
And he dreamed, and behold a ladder set up on the
earth, and the top of it reached to heaven: and behold
the angels of God ascending and descending on it.
And, behold, the LORD stood above it, and said, I am
the LORD God of Abraham thy father, and the God
of Isaac: the land whereon thou liest, to thee will I
give it, and to thy seed.

(GENESIS 28:11–13, KJV)

Preview

...yea, thou shalt lie down
and thy sleep shalt be sweet.
(Proverbs 3:24)

ALL OF US have an inner life. Do we call that our soul? Our psyche? Our seat of sensibility? Perhaps spirit. Whatever our language for that unseen world, it is often secret. Hidden. Some of us are richly aware of our inner lives, others are only dimly so.

For one who grows aware, there comes tremendous potential power—both spiritual *and* practical power—to be and live out the beauty of who one really is. That seed of power involves a different dimension from everyday life, and yet should we nurture that seed it controls the material world around us. This happens somewhat inexplicably—unlike earth's cause and effect, not as we usually perceive things. That's because the spiritual controls the physical. Even if incomprehensibly. *Even in sleep.*

First, let's consider prayer. That's part of our inner life—usually considered to be largely an interior action. Closely held by most; linked to daily outcomes for believers; highly instrumental in the sort of transcendent realms and dreams we shall discuss.

All of us pray—some, pray to God.[1] Others: who can say? For all those who scoff, who insist, "There is no God. Prove He exists, then I'll listen," I repeat author Frederick Buechner's idea:

In our human tent, trying to prove God's existence is like Sherlock Holmes trying to demonstrate the existence of Arthur Conant Doyle.[2]

A popular television show reinforces the point—and sets my stage of exploration of the spiritual power of our interior life. When a cunning, charming, conniving politician meets a rare moment of conscience, he begins to pray along these lines: He says he prays just *to* himself, and he prays just *for* hmself. None of that compassionate hogwash for him.[3]

Was the scene meant to shock and dismay us? Is it worth debating the existence of God with one of that mentality? Not many have a heart that's as hard as that fellow. Nevertheless, in a crisis, even he turns inward. Alas, that character was

---

1 Self-existent, omnipresent, omniscient, omnipotent Source, Creator, Creative Intelligence, Supreme Being, the Divine Love.
2 Frederick Buechner, *Wishful Thinking* (Harper & Row, New York.)
3 *House of Cards*. 2013. Netflix original series. (Paraphrased)

unreceptive to his highest sensibilities. Fortunately, most of us are more open.

Just as more and more collective conversations—in films and television and daily life—involve our subjective field, so more and more of us sense something real, something guiding, entirely legitimate, is going on within us—again, even in sleep.

Most mass media these days discusses our inner life in some way because that inner something is our shared experience. We all feel, wish, worry, enjoy, dream. Some of us dream lavishly; some sparingly. Some slumber mostly unaware. A few sleep "wide-awake." Many of us not only remember our dreams, it's as if there's also a kind of prayer going on as we sleep and dream. I call that "*transcendent sleep*"—it's when during our slumbers, there's a communion between the soul and the Divine—as if even while asleep we are "sealed with the Spirit of promise." Is that not our *sweetest sleep?* It's the time when, while resting, we are nevertheless working out how to live to the praise of God's glory. (Eph. 1:12-13) I suppose this book is written especially for those of us who yearn to enhance that work.

And it *does* take work—mostly a new posture of heart—to do so.

Which does not mean that we must be (or that more and more of us are) formally religious. To the contrary. Huge droves of us are fleeing organized religion. Non-denominational and interdenominational groups are burgeoning. Our turn away from traditions may mean we are growing *whole*—which, to me, means growing into a state where we see that, in God, there is "no difference between us." (Rom. 10:12) Listen to a few Sunday sermons and you'll hear a trend toward fresh compassion, acceptance of people with diverse faiths, cultures, lifestyles.

A Personal Aside

Your author has spent her life largely outside the doors of organized religion. Yet, her life's path became deeply religious in both a traditional, and a more radical, transcendence that called her away from many conventional norms. Even in childhood, direct experience –encounter– said: God is alive, here, now—with us. Later came her turn to fairly orthodox viewpoints. And, thus, her love of this book's central premise: God speaks to us day *and* night, through every channel, even in some of our sanctified dreams.

If, like me, you sense that you live in a living, breathing, infinitely intelligent Love and *conscious* Reality, read on. That living Love obliges me to share this message in as broad a way as possible. For the most part, I'll use my language;

please translate it into yours. For in God, we are One, and yet as with language and perceptions, each is distinctive.

Our Spiritual Fingerprint Matters

When it comes to spirituality, each of us is highly individual. Ours may be an orthodox faith, but from birth we possess a unique spiritual fingerprint.[4] Nowhere is that truer than with dreams. If we are receptive, certain infrequent dreams can lead to time-honored religious understandings, values, and growth in the "peace that passes understanding." The holy dream can direct even the most cynical disbeliever to an epiphany of deep faith, and convict such a one of errors, guilt, and sin.

You could say, "Well, there's nothing in my religious beliefs that leads me to consider dreams as 'holy.'"

To that I repeat Pastor Oswald Chambers' century-old idea: There is no more inconsistent pattern than that which our Lord reflects. He worked on the Sabbath; He spoke of righteousness, yet sat down with the disreputable. Study and see! We must be vigilant not to make "a fetish of consistency."[5] Apart from the great commandment, Jesus

---

4 M. Sinetar, *Spiritual Intelligence* (Maryknoll, NY: Orbis, 2007).

5 Oswald Chambers, *My Utmost for His Highest* (Urichsville, OH: Barbour Books & Co., 1987), 319. (The Scottish-born Chambers died in 1917.)

gave us no formulas. Plus, much of what he taught referred to the inner life—the inner man of the heart.

Since these are heavy, heady themes, this little book will lead to many questions to help you consider your own direct experience. Perhaps you'll keep a journal or discuss these notions with your most trusted, qualified spiritual and religious confidants. Our lives involve both linear and asymmetrical experience; rational and so-called irrational, atypical ideas. Follow your deepest heart—that "small, still voice within"—to explore your experiences. Dreams embrace all of the spiritual and religious field, and more. Understood rightly, many dreams open our door to true learning.

Our True Learning

Having meditated on variants of these themes for years, I must pause for a moment to make a distinction: I shall deliberately, in what follows, avoid mention of visions. To me, visions are a related, but separate, issue.[6]

---

6 As discussed in these pages, and briefly put, a *dream* is an interior image, picture, story etc., apprehended during sleep. A *vision (horama)* is a spectacle, appearance, sight, perhaps apparition appearing externally. A vision can result from ingesting drugs (e.g., LSD), plants (e.g., peyote), or having certain mental instabilities, chemical imbalances, etc. The dream is universal: the world over, people dream and nightly. Only a few of us have ever had visions. See also W.E. Vines, *Expository Dictionary of New Testament Words* (Nashville, Tn., Thomas Nelson. 3rd Printing),1202.

While originally I designed these ideas as a pastoral resource, I heard that a much wider audience would be interested. When in dialogue with like-minded, trustworthy friends, qualified counselors and colleagues—or more privately, on our own—we can explore a dream's meanings. Literal interpretations are probably easy, but questionable.

Although the holy dream stands center stage on these pages, the purpose of *most* dreams is practical; they are received to be integrated into daily life. But let us stay with holy— spiritually wholesome—dreams. For openers, we might wonder what constitutes that spiritual wholeness?

I use the phrase *spiritual wholeness* to speak of the holiness born *only* of God. In part, *holiness* means separated unto God. The sanctified dream moves us in that direction. It guides; it corrects; it directs us to our helpful, contributive life with others. It's practical and usually points us toward righteous choices. All have work to do in everyday matters to satisfy that purpose. Fulfilling our life's reason involves true learning, the discovery of who we are and how we're meant to live, love, contribute to self-and-other. If we solve that, we've hit the jackpot.

Dream or no dream, we are, I believe, born to infuse our world—whatever it is today—with the climate of the Celestial, not in some ethereal way, but where the rubber meets the road of our daily doings. In our midst—at work, at home, at family gatherings, there is usually someone who adds value, who exudes a quiet joy, or is kind or hopeful. That someone often reflects a rich, loving, inner life—not in a phony piety or tedious artificial cheerfulness, but actually, authentically.

However, some say it's impossible for us, as imperfect humans, to be holy. Lest we become hard-hearted types who grouse and nitpick at everyone's foibles, or struggle and strain to perfect ourselves, let's remember that God's holy ones are usually the seemingly hopeless cases who ride into towns on donkeys, go against the grain of convention, get laughed at. Or are feared, despised, crucified.

It's clear: we don't perfect ourselves or earn our way into heaven. Any good we reflect is God's good. That is why we can use our most spiritual dreams to infuse God's touch on us into our life with others.

Holy Dreams as Heightened Awareness: Two Parts

Because all this is so subtle and multifaceted, I've divided this book into two parts. Part I, introduces and outlines the lay of the land of *holy dreams*. I offer sample dreams to shed light on some of these encounters, and list a few characteristics of holy dreams. Part II, then, fills in that picture with more, mostly adapted, but specific, samples of holy dreams, ideas about using Scripture, and a few word-study illustrations. These underscore the spiritual, I believe, timeless elements we can discover in such dreams. Also, because there are few more fulfilling conversations than those we can have with, say, a skilled professional or trusted other about this topic, I've included some notions related to the reciprocity of that dialogue.[7]

Throughout I'll ask the sorts of questions that I ask myself. For instance, are there links between the minds of those in highly creative fields, like the arts, and those with a religious vocation? If so, what are some of these, and how might they relate to sleep, to renewal, and to cultivating the rich interior life that I sense summons to all of us holy or other dreams?

And, continually, as I wrote this book, I wondered why so little has been said about these subjects and also, …

If everything in Creation speaks of the Creator and the Celestial, why not the holy dream?

Through expanded awareness in daily life *and* in the holy dream, we can turn with single-minded intent to the true

7 It's usual in books like this for readers to ask how and where to find exemplary professionals who facilitate dialogue as described in these chapters. This author does not make recommendations, but has met highly skilled facilitators teaching courses on a variety of related themes at many universities. Also our local places of worship are often good sources for that sort of information and inquiry.

substance of faith that leads so beautifully to *Christ's* wholeness—not our human perfection. We are *being with* the One Who is *being with* us—not trying to be flawless or worthy.

To shed light on that idea, consider a "one minute wisdom" told by renowned storyteller—and story gatherer—Father Anthony De Mello:

There was once a charismatic preacher who taught her students, "A few of you think that we must *put* God into our lives. Not so. He is already here—with us, everywhere. There is no place or time God is not." And then she added, "It's our job to realize that."[8]

Don't such realizations come both slowly and suddenly, while shopping for grapes or painting a fence post? Or dreaming?

Why wouldn't God be communing with us through both waking and sleeping consciousness? And why couldn't we, at least occasionally, receive sacred messages in our dreams? I propose we can and do discern God's touch while asleep, and that we can learn to recall—even invite—such dreams. And in time and with mature *spiritual* intelligence, we can learn to speak and understand a transcendent dream's sweet, Celestial language. That's what this book is about. So let us explore.

———

8 Anthony De Mello, *One Minute Wisdom* (Image Books, 1985), 130. (Paraphrased)

Part I

...Awake, thou that sleepest
Arise from the dead, And Christ
shall give thee light.
(EPHESIANS 5:14)

CHAPTER 1

Our *True* Learning

As for these four children, God gave them knowledge
and skill in all learning and wisdom; and Daniel had
understanding in all visions and dreams.
(DANIEL 1:17)

THE ENTIRE BIBLE seems a series of lessons in true learning.
The biblical prophet Daniel's spiritual gifts prove the point.
His inborn gifts let him "speak" a heavenly language. He saw
into the very nature of things, even ephemeral things like
the meaning of dreams. The Hebrew patriarch Jacob serves
as another example. His daily preoccupations must have led
his mind's eye into the Kingdom within during sleep, as he
watched God's holy angels climbing up to heaven and down
again. (See Gen. 28:10–19)

Neither Daniel nor Jacob had a "dream dictionary"; neither man had attended weekend seminars on dream interpretations. Yet they understood. How is that possible when

3

we—with our wealth of spiritual resources and all manner of liberties to explore ideas, hear from and exchange viewpoints with experts—have fallen so far away from those divine realms? Understanding ideas about the Spirit[9] or spiritual things generally is only possible with God's grace on us—because what is impossible to us, is possible for God, for Whom *all things* are possible. (Luke 18:27) If there is an attribute common to all the Bible's heroes and heroines, it is the *receptivity to* the things of God. In part, that quality is also a skill; it can be developed.[10]

As Jacob heard the Lord's words, wouldn't he have *had* to receive the message? Isn't discernment also a skill, an essential aspect of receptivity? Jacob's yielding and discernment unfolded his life's destiny—its import and significance to the future. Surely, both receptivity and discernment are capacities that help us grow whole. True learning births that sort of growth—the wisdom that paves our way to being creative contributors to our own and others' lives.

---

9 I define the word "spirit" as does the dictionary: *animating essence.*

10 Elsewhere, I have called that receptivity the feminine principle. Others have, too. I believe most in the arts or inventive fields and many with a religious call have it: It's when we receive, or yield to, the Source of our inner life. (For me, God.) The pattern also seems contemplative. Mary of Bethany received a lasting, heart-altering friendship with Jesus and, like his mother Mary, she seems to have pondered deeply and continuously the things of God. See: M. Sinetar, *Posture of Heart:* The Mary Pattern. (Monograph, Sinetar (*Teleios*) Center. www.marshasinetar.com., 2008)

Why can't we, as ordinary people, also trust a certain sort of dream to invite such intelligence? That's not precisely book smarts or scientific expertise. It's more like illumination – some inmost light bulb turning on. Illumination, I suspect, is one link between the creative mind and the religious: The "Aha!" moment that all of us experience and no doubt enjoy, seems more likely to occur in inventive types and in those with a religious bent.

I must add, and might repeat, that of course creative people are often very religious and religious people are often very creative. Because this isn't always the case and because the holy dream can benefit all types of people I'll separate the "types" for the purposes of discussion.

As the divine love infuses us with all manner of wisdom in the holy dream, we *can* learn to discern meaning and, with that, perhaps receive more "Aha!" moments.

These dreams are filled with truths about who we are created to be. And because holy dreams flow from the presence of the divine love to all who dream—even once—in that fashion somehow and necessarily they contribute to the greater good. *All* can contribute: a circus clown, a UPS driver, a parent, a plumber, a so-called bum. Contribution seems a second link between creative and religious endeavors. In later chapters, we'll examine a few things that enhance that contributive result. And, yes, the holy dream is one.

God's grace relates to wisdom, to receiving wisdom, and to cultivating intuitive skills such as Daniel possessed when interpreting celestial "visions and dreams." All this is spiritual. All this starts with—and flows from—God. All this involves true learning, not precisely academic achievement.

We don't give so much as a glance in God's direction without His grace. Yet, surely our prayers and preoccupations till the soil of consciousness. We choose, each day, with what engagements to tangle. *We choose the contents of our mind.*

Jacob, for example, might not have dreamt of ladders and angels or heard the Lord's voice had he not somehow been pondering his situation or been touched by God to apprehend that message. We are called to holy dreaming, just as we are called to true learning. This seems a kind of silent dance to an inaudible refrain. We sense a movement or quickening in our Partner, then we step in that direction. In this scenario, to dance well, we must tune into our inmost sensibility. Then *we* choose what steps to take, or what content of mind to serve. (Josh. 24:15)

What's Our Most Creative, Practical Lesson?

Answer: *True* learning, or the growth and grasp of whatever helps us understand how to be and how to live out the conscious, beautiful, and *authentic* being we were created to be. If, as I do, you believe and trust Genesis 1:26–27, that God made us in His own image and likeness, then it follows that there is something lovely, loving, and worthwhile for each of us to be and do. It's our job to discover it. Such is the way of faith, effort and ultimate fruitfulness.

There is, for instance, a vast divide of learning between the man or woman who feels – senses – an inner prompt to practice medicine, who *love*s the notion of being trusted and healing others, and the one who enters the field of medicine because of parental pressure or a desire for prestige and wealth. The first, with a perhaps excited use of all available resources, including books, schooling, jobs and experience, grows in healing skill and acumen. The second one, with perhaps an odd sense of loss or struggle, wonders why the journey feels so joyless, so empty. Each one's discovery or questions, each one's answers will be very different. True learning is infinitely individual.

Some dreams (and not only "holy" ones) point us to our valid life-path and purpose –that's a learning that seems our most critical task. Whatever relationships, career, vocation, joys and hardships we experience, all of that and more can help us grow. Usually, a good, long lifetime lets us complete our course. The holy dream can guide and teach us. Shortly, we'll look at what characterizes these dreams.

Daniel's courage, his truthful stance when speaking to those with power and authority, were all part of his life's charter, his inborn destiny. We cannot separate holy dreams from true learning. One begets the other.

Just as Daniel's wisdom and skills opened up holy dreams, increased his spiritual intelligence, and gave him power to be who he was, so our wisdom, tenacity and power come as we risk understanding our inner life and gain courage to complete the race *we* were born to run.

How do we cultivate such wisdom? First, as Jesus taught, we'll need to seek out the Kingdom within. Eventually, as later chapters show, we can grasp *hidden* certainties that empower us. These invigorate our very life.

At the seat of every Spirit-filled soul, there lives an instinctive drive—a spiritual impulse, a lift of consciousness—to wake up from life's illusions. That urge searches out everything for ways to be free of bondage to false gods and sensory, materialistic traps. That prompt also seems the start of our tendency toward spiritual *wholeness—separation unto God*. We'll define that tendency in many different ways. If we simply look around our neighborhoods, place of work, our families, we'll probably spot someone who seems to live "separated unto God."

All our earthly forms and expressions—art, music, relationships, nature, and today even technology—can further that awakening. And some dreams do as well, especially if one is open to a dream's language.

Vast Potential for Spiritual Growth

Questions spring from these ideas on dreams. For example:

1. How do *you* define the word spiritual?
2. What does the phrase "spiritual wholeness" mean to you?
3. Do you believe it's possible for a human—a flawed creature, living in a flawed world—to grow toward spiritual wholeness? If so, can you think of examples? What might that growth entail?

I urge you to mull over your own answers to all such questions, to find your *own* truths: This is the way of *true* learning. It's how we open the door to authenticity. We know from experience that the more we abandon our true nature, the louder grows our squeaking wheel of sorrow in all its forms and variants – psychological and spiritual.

Our Inborn Celestial Language

It's been said that art and music are appreciated only by intuiting, perhaps learning, the special celestial language "of the spheres." To me, most dreams speak to us in the same sort of tongue. A Miro painting or one by a child –a preschooler, possibly before he or she has been programmed into the color-within-the-lines school of art -- seem full of dreamlike scenes. Since there is much to discover in all of these areas, more questions arise:

- To what extent could the words, colors, images, landscapes or picturesque messages of certain dreams be *God's* language?
- To what extent could the holy dream be a much ignored, highly individuated spiritual code?
- To what extent could some seemingly ordinary dreams point us to our day-to-day spiritual "homework?"

As an example of that homework, when one person dreamt of his own death, at first he was frightened. After reading up on the *psychology* of dreams, he discovered that most such dreams are not prophetic but rather *spiritual*: they can signify transformation, the dropping of one phase or season or character trait for another—the growth into more wholesome, truthful expressions. What he had learned from his dream while asleep, he now had to put into new and more honest and beautiful forms or manifestations in daily life. This what I mean by "homework."

Only for People "of Faith"?

Christians call the Holy Spirit the aspect of God that inspires, comforts and guides us. Does the Holy Spirit comfort, guide, and draw us into our wholeness only if we are people "of faith"? It may seem as if our exploration would solely suit believers. But *no,* holy dreams are not sent to an exclusive club; God is calling to *each* of us, all the time. Who's to say how and when He addresses us?

Do we interpret dreams psychologically? Do we find such spiritual ideas ridiculous? No matter. If you are open-hearted, secure enough to consider your deeper, most powerful, and atypical interior experience, you may find amazing value in certain dreams. That's especially true for anyone hungry for spiritual direction. Returning to ideas mentioned earlier, even world-weary people want life-answers.

For instance, culture—our collective mind-set—says a lot about us: Thus, again I turn to media: The major characters in the popular television series, *Damages* (FX; Netflix) were haunted by nightmares. The scenes, stories, symbolism of these torturous dreams lingered throughout the characters' lives, following them throughout the show. That suggests that we—the collective viewer—accept as natural to look to (or away from) dreams for the deepest, unexamined traumas and heartaches of life. In dreams, our conscience shows us what we may avoid knowing.

It takes *spiritual* sensibility, to appreciate the power, message, and occasional poignancy of dream sequences. I believe that is a sensitization process. And expressions such as in art, poetry, film—drama of all sorts—literature, and psychoanalysis show us that millions, if not all of us, have such sensitivity and encounter such dream sequences.

By contrast, dreams can seem useless, simply fanciful, for the less spiritual, for more rigid, linear or conventional minds. I've known students and business leaders who seemed to distrust their softer, more flexible or uncertain side—all part of the unknown of creativity, and the ineffable aspect of dreams. Perhaps some of us have been hurt or hardened particularly by early punitive or legalistic training.

For Your Consideration

My bias seems clear. However, the present exploration is for *your* study, for further dialogue with your most trusted others. Your pastor, priest, rabbi, chaplain, spiritual director or counselor usually can help unravel knotty issues that dreams may reveal. We discuss this later.

Consult your highest wisdom—your thoughts and interior guidance on the subject. All of that seems well worth the effort you may invest in such learning, which can include note-taking right after a memorable dream, journaling, readings on related subjects. When it comes to learning, the sky's the limit.

In the Orthodox Study Bible, the Psalmist offers a lovely version of Psalm 139:11: "...the night shall be light to my delight."[11]

Consider this: While most of us are largely unconscious during our slumbers, for the Psalmist even the darkness sheds light: His seemed an instinctual religious sensibility, completely open to his inner life, and the Kingdom within.

That impulse obliges the Psalmist—as it may some of us—to dig deeply into his psyche for any particle of Godly wisdom.

Praying at night or at dawn, meditation[12] and reveries of all sorts, help us remain open to the interior, frequently celestial, language of certain dreams. We "chew" on them afterwards, while washing dishes, driving to work, clipping our nails, pouring tea for a friend.

In sum, God's eternal impartations are never confined to waking consciousness, to mere daylight, or to Old Testament

---

11   *The Orthodox Study Bible-Old Testament Text* (St. Athanasius Academy of Orthodox Theology: St. Athanasius Academy Septuagint, 2008).

12   There are so many meditative practices, most quite subtle, quite powerful. The Psalmists seemed to meditate on Scripture; other methods – like tinkering with the breath – could require a preliminary discussion with one's health care professional.

prophets. Surely, we are created for the images and unfolding awareness of the Transcendent at *all* times. Surely, today vast numbers of openhearted, faithful sorts experience the Light—illumination—by which the soul unites with God.

And I say more: Everyone—not just the faithful – can experience the Light that is our very Life. (John 1:4) Every dream, not just a holy one, that lingers, troubles, confounds, comforts, or repeats its message seems a call to pay attention, to discern what's deeply hidden within us. These messages are like clear, cool water to the parched.

For now, consider how all sorts of contemplative activities such as prayer, the slow and thoughtful study of Scripture, even chance remarks from strangers, can witness to the Spirit's prompts, and give us pause to think things over. These prompts come when they will. Noticing what's happening within and without is our job and it's contemplative. We, it must be said, are born to heed and heed diligently. So comes true learning.

———

CHAPTER 2

"Awakening" in Sleep

And be renewed in the spirit of your mind...
(EPHESIANS 4:23)

AFTER YEARS OF business successes, a high achieving, socially adroit executive took a radical turn toward a solitary, reflective life. He moved from a bustling city to a farming community.

Today, he considers himself a self-styled and "casual" contemplative.[13] At first, however, his simple, peaceful life ushered in many unknowns: The loss of old friends, the realities of inconveniences, the need to budget carefully and unfamiliar surroundings.

Before, money had flowed freely. Now, frugality was his norm. He experienced highs and lows, felt chaotic as fear and excitement mingled. These disruptions invited the following dream:

---

13 See M. Sinetar, *Sometimes, Enough is Enough* (New York: St Martin's Press, 2007).

I am tidying up my garden, wearing a torn, grimy sweatshirt with holes in it, and torn grubby sweatpants. It's hot. I'm sweating, disheveled. The garden, however, is looking tidy, lush and green. Suddenly, I hear a motor. Here comes a black, old-style English taxi-cab, at the top of my driveway— the sort of vintage car you'd see in a classic British film.

Out climbs the most elegant, beautiful man I'd ever seen. Tall, confident, self-possessed. He's wearing an immaculate white linen suit, and strolls gracefully down my dusty drive. I try to hide. He sees everything, including me. Thankfully, he is kind: Eyeing my scruffy garb, he says, in droll Noel Coward tones, 'Well, you've been working hard—It's good. All is well.'

Or, words to that effect. My heart knows he's right. All is well.

What Characterizes the "Holy" Dream?

That sample dream helps pinpoint some features of our holiest dreams. (To drive home these ideas, I'll repeat some of them as we go.)

The dream above and the dreamer's response to it captures a few important elements. Speaking generally, in sleep our human *spirit* can be awakened by the indwelling Holy Spirit—the Spirit of God. Some call that consciousness, or the Light—or prompts of the divine love. Choose your own language. That quickening happens in the spirit of *our* mind.

And...

- No matter how corrective, guiding, or cautioning the holy dream, it always renews us—to repeat—"in the spirit of our mind." (Eph. 4:23)

As the dreamer above noted,

In my heart, I knew all was well.

- Unlike "natural" dreams, holy dreams seem to be somewhat coherent—more like parables, they tell a story, carry a hopeful, directing or cautionary message, teach a lesson, renew us somehow.

Thus the dreamer reports,

> *I wake up, feeling greatly blessed, if also bewildered. What did that dream mean? I knew the Man was holy (even in sleep, I see Him as Christ or symbolizing the Lord). Someone has called Jesus 'the sacred Guest of the Soul' and my Visitor fits that bill.*

- We may not understand the dream's import quickly. Years could pass without a clue. Yet, we are comforted, warned, taught a lesson, restored. Something good—fruitful—happens. Time and experience let us grasp the dream's deep meanings:

In the dreamer's words...

> *When fully awake, I sensed all my changes were right—despite seeming disorder... in the spirit of my mind, or heart, I am reinvigorated—restored. Is that garden part of me?*

- Just as Scripture's stories contain countless layers of importance, so do holy dreams. We recall these dreams—usually for a lifetime.

Just so. The dreamer marvels at that lasting quality.

I've never forgotten that dream. Now, when my faith falters, I recall my Guest's words, 'All is well,' and am renewed.

Part II expands on these themes. For instance, we'll see how, as a Catholic priest, Saint John Bosco's dreams were of such an enduring nature that he traveled around, teaching his students about his dreams' lessons. Here is another characteristic of the holy dream: Over time, somehow it profits others *through* us.

Contemplation, perhaps trustworthy spiritual direction—not precisely *self*-help—unfolds the substance of the things of God. The holy dream reveals God's *nature* and purposes. Confucius was said to have taught that reflection (i.e., contemplation) is the mind's noblest learning task. Holy dreams deserve that nobility of thought.

Furthermore, all dreams can teach us a new language about who we are. If we study Scripture contemplatively, it's usual for a line or verse to pop into our mind as we ponder the holy dream. This is another issue we revisit more illustratively in Part II.

And more: reflection after such dreams can clarify…

- Our faith, the gifts and fruit of the Spirit.
- God's attributes, for me, as Father, Son, and Holy Spirit; for others, maybe a revived sense of love,

awareness—the hope and surge of optimism of being "led" by beneficent, if invisible, forces.

- The spiritual message of the dream, itself
- The words, images, and symbols that we receive, especially if something in these reflect the lessons of Scripture and/or other holy issues that apply. Even colors convey messages.

In such dreams, a restructuring or remodeling of consciousness takes place. The so-called irrational blends with, informs and perhaps shifts the rational. Insight lifts the curtain of unawareness to reveal new understandings. The fixtures of our old—fleshly—thoughts are thrown out, moved, changed. Our "inner man"[14] is, to a degree, waking up—although our outer self sleeps. Some say every character in a dream represents us, as dreamers. Others say the people in our dreams mirror *parts* of us. Others say otherwise.

It may further discernment of a dream to notice the *sense* we have of ourselves, after the dream. We can pay attention to its tone or ambiance or our feelings to fathom initial meanings.

Let's say we have felt off-balance, as did our dreamer in that earlier sample. We might dream about living in a house built

---

14 Some of us are touchy about words with gender implications: If we wince at the term "man" or even "inner man" it may help to know that many people interpret *man* as *manifestation*— perhaps a neutral clarification.

on an actual rock. Or, instead, we might dream of a friend living on sand. Such details could seem obvious, nevertheless the sense we'll have after waking up is telling. The first dream leaves us with a sense of stability. It could mean that's what we're seeking, since we've been feeling unstable. After the second dream, we feel something might slip. The tone of the dream leaves us shaky, insecure. Perhaps for all our apparent success, we need to build real substance into our lives with better choices – in conduct, friends, work, spending habits—that are reliable, based on core values of real worth. That is what I mean by *sense*.

If we've felt down in the dumps or ill, our dreams could be full of healing symbols, beautiful birds, water or gardens. However basic, this illustrates the point. Our *awareness* of things, what these mean to us, seems a reasonable starting point for discernment.

For Your Consideration

Relating to our first dream example: What methods of understanding have been helpful for you? How might diverse counselors or religious professionals help themselves (and/or us) more effectively interpret seemingly holy dreams in spiritual—less psychological—ways?

Some regenerative ideas of holiness bring us as dreamers into certain Kingdom realities. For instance, a few universal themes (that our sample dreams illustrate) include such things as our gaining...

- a wholly new identity and *spiritual* restoration, in Christ,
- a more refined aesthetic and/or lovely image of Truth—the holy dream invites discernment of the Beauty of holiness,
- a wholesome authority from Above, not of our "small self."[15]

Every powerful dream is transformative in some fashion. Yet, while the usual psychology of consciousness seems to promote self-help methods of transformation (e.g., positive thinking, cognitive therapies, visualizations, affirmations, guided meditation), and while these methods can be extremely effective for some in raising awareness, modifying thought and behavior, such techniques are humanly directed. They begin with the creature *trying* to get better, improve, heal, grow whole. The holy dream differs somewhat.

Here we come to a slippery-slope since self-effort is required in life; of course we must choose in right (i.e., righteous) directions if we're to live well; naturally, that involves

---

15 M. Sinetar, *Ordinary People as Monks & Mystics*. Revised with Preface (Mahwah, NJ. Paulist Press, 2007).

our good sense, energy, exertion. However, in the framework under exploration, it's the Spirit during sleep and dreams guiding us, raising awareness, not our "fleshly" self. After all, we're asleep.

Recalling Jacob's dream of that ladder, those angels climbing up to heaven and down to earth again and his hearing the Lord speak to him: there comes a time of waking up, of being faced with the choice to *welcome* or reject the import of what's been experienced in sleep.

More food for thought or dialogue that might increase clarity. Some seemingly ordinary dreams also raise life's big questions: why are we alive? What's our purpose? Why did we dream about death, failure or forgiveness? These sorts of inquiries could help us reach a point where, like Jacob did, we choose consciously a more rigorous path. In all its aspects, the holy dream quickens us, could well lead to deliberate choices (or lively deliberations) related to improving something in our everyday life.

We are still only talking about dreams. Even so, mundane, but life affirming, choices can flow out of our receptivity to certain impressions in a dream. Which seems a cooperative play between God and ourselves, not exactly *our* good idea.

In John 5:19, Jesus says he does nothing of himself, but only what he sees his Father do. What do you think that "seeing" entails?

Doesn't a kind of spiritual intelligence alert us during and/ or after a forceful dream? Somehow, we are being sensitized to the dream's intent. If it's spiritual, it's likely our heightened sensitivity is a result of the Lord's touch, presence and dream communiqué. All that starts with God—not man. We're simply being urged into a higher dimension, a kind of revealing, a primal Reality (or Kingdom) transpiring within. Moreover, with apologies for asking the obvious: mustn't one be supremely stable, lucid and emotionally mature to interpret any dream? These states, however, are tough to judge when it comes to others.

Parents are known to wake up in the middle of the night for no earthly reason. They've sensed they must look in on their children. When they do, they may discover a fire, a burglar or a feverish youngster. Or, they see that everything is perfectly fine.

What sort of impulse woke them up? Was it irrational? Maybe a different type of rationality? Is sanity always rational? Those sorts of questions seem related to our inner life, our dream life, our daily life.

With a holy dream the Spirit of Truth awakens us on the inside, first *perceptually*, in thought, motivation and awareness. Initially, this is more akin to being "raised up," as Scripture puts it, in consciousness—*rather than* some intellectual or cognitive operation. We probably don't ever theorize our way into a spiritual awakening. Still, as an aftermath of such dreams there usually are choices to make. Even choosing to read this or that book or attend this or that film can be a turning point.

Speaking through the Psalmist, the Lord says, "I removed his shoulder from the burden; his hands were delivered from the pots." (Ps. 81:6)

Our burdens may stay where they are. Our pots and floors still need scrubbing. Yet we sense improvement. We *are* better; in a tangible way, we are at ease. God frees our human shoulder, but not always our human efforts. Things may look the same in the natural realm, but—within—our bondage has been lifted. We, the human person, didn't lift our own weights.

So in the holy dream: We are led out of Egypt (i.e., captivity) by God's thought *with us,* His secret language in a dream blends with our thought. This is so even when we hear—apprehend—but do not understand. (Ps. 81:5)

Holy Dreams Lift "the Veil"

In a metaphorical sense, "veil" means that covering over our illusory or materialistic perspective. When the veil lifts, spiritual darkness fades in the Light of Truth; our inner eyes start to see "in a new and living way." (Heb.10:20)

That illumination can, and often does, happen with the holy dream.

To repeat: Every night does not bring holy dreams. The saintly—like John Bosco—are unusually gifted in that respect. Just as architects are sensitive to form and design, the spiritually gifted are alert to the things of God. They are, to me, spiritual artists, exceptionally attuned to inner Light, to the lifting of the "veil."[16]

How sad that our highly gifted *spiritual* youngsters, our sensitive sons and daughters, our young, aspiring religious are not culturally encouraged along saintly lines. Are they taught about other types of creative people? Are they shown likenesses between their gifts and those of others? Our conventional world often shuns their calling.[17]

For fifty years, John Bosco dreamt so vividly along Spirit-filled lines that he awoke exhausted. For most of us, in contrast, the sacred messages of night are few and far between. That cannot be said too often, given our too-human propensity for self-adulation and drama.

---

16 In Scripture, the "veil" could also mean *flesh,* as in the flesh of Jesus which he willingly gave up for our salvation so that we might know a "new and living way."

17 One encouragement for young people considering a religious vocation is their reading about the saints. And learning from ordinary men and women who reflect simple goodness in everyday life. For that encouragement, I love Robert Ellsberg's beautiful book, *All Saints* (Crossroad. New York. 1998) which considers the lavish diversity of those who walk in Truth.

Yet, sacred dreams, though atypical, are as holy for each of us as, say, Jacob's dream was for him. And, they are not born of *our* carnal mind. Before sleep, Jacob put his head on a stone. In a metaphorical sense, "stone" means the substance or foundation of Truth. That suggests that Jacob, before sleep, prepared himself for some higher, finer thought *during* sleep. Which seems a sensible practice (a sort of entreaty) of those tending toward holiness. Day and night, there can be prayer, even if merely an eye-blink in God's direction. Our preoccupations tend to influence dreams. Here's an example that demonstrates the creative wealth awaiting us in dreams:

A frugal housekeeper, furious about the flimsy quality of high cost, stove-burner shields that she favored, got a notion stuck in her mind that there must be a better, less expensive way to a clean stove top. Every time she cleaned her stove, she meditated on solutions. One night she dreamt ("for hours") that she was soaking the burner shields in a natural food supplement that she consumed daily.[18] In the morning she rushed to test the dream-idea. "It worked! It's not perfect, but the grease just melts away and the substance doesn't tear the fragile shields like scouring pads do. I figure I'll save about eighty dollars a year on scouring pads." The process is the

18 Of course, we do not recommend acting on any dream-idea containing such specific data without first checking with the appropriate expert(s) and/or manufacturer.

point. Meditation on an idea supports the idea, draws it out of us.

Undeniably, that dream shows us the influence of thought – be it on Scripture or scouring pads– on dreams. I leave to you whether or not the dream just mentioned was spiritual.

Our topic, seen through the filter of spiritual wholeness, transcends psychology. However, it must be said there is a fine line between psychology and spirituality.

Some of our most creative citizens—actors, artists, inventors, homemakers—can be our least "well-adjusted" citizens: perhaps idiosyncratic, solitary, cantankerous, absent-minded, preoccupied with their engagements.

With that in mind, our samples demonstrate that most sacred dreams will …

(a) bypass some psychological terms, *yet*
(b) often echo psychology's lessons, and
(c) adhere to the idea of holiness as a viable life option—the only practical, obligatory way of *being*—and not a delusional pipe dream. (Isn't that what Scripture tells us?)

For those who love God above all, and strive to love neighbors as themselves, the *holy* dream furthers His message.

That also means occasionally in such matters we turn to trusted, qualified others for greater understanding.

Intuitions, inspirations, the life-changing, life-saving idea involves *spiritual intelligence*: The celestial, God-with-us Presence expressing through our humanly-occupied thought, giving way to daydreams and night dreams. These can awaken our "new man," our true man[19]

Scripture describes ordinary sorts who, while in the Spirit, receive leadings of pure truth from God, both day and night, so that "old things pass away" and our "new man" is enlivened. (2 Cor. 5:17) Thus, Paul's admonitions…

…be renewed in the spirit of your mind.

And…put on the new man, which after God is created in righteousness and true holiness. (Eph. 4:23–24)

———

One Enduring Bias

I've always emphasized one point: More people than we commonly recognize are putting on the new man. Like an unfamiliar suit of clothes, initially that outfit can feel tight,

19 See for example, Emanuel Swedenborg's accounts, in his many books, of his dreams, the angelic world, his ideas of the true, the good; e.g., *Heaven and Hell*; *Divine Love and Wisdom*.

uncomfortable. Thankfully, when in the Spirit we transcend the feelings of "the flesh."

The fourth century poet-theologian, St. Ephrem's term "Robe of Glory," describes in familiar concepts God's gift of enabling us to put on Christ. The poet uses everyday ideas to boost our comprehension of what we've been given.

St. Ephrem's hymnal, *Paradise,* is dreamlike. He echoes St. Paul with a vocabulary borrowed from our idea of clothing to convey the magnificence of God's grace:

> Do not let your intellect be disturbed
> by mere names;
> For Paradise has simply clothed itself
> in terms that are akin to you;
> it is not because it is impoverished
> that it put on your imagery;
> rather, your nature is far too weak
> to be able to attain its greatness...[20]

Just so: *Because* our human nature is so weak, so easily seduced by outer influences, dreams show us what we are too closed or cowardly to grasp. Sleep can be a poetic time, a time when, in the *spirit* of our mind, pictures, stories, colors transport us

---

20 St. Ephrem the Syrian, trans. Stephen Brock, *Hymns on Paradise* (Crosswood, NY: St. Vladimir's Press, 1990), 48.

softly, silently, into transcendent spheres of light-filled learning. The holy dream's animating essence can guide, restore and comfort. In the sleep that is sweet, God speaks to us of our true identity. And pierces the dark, veiled corners of our mind with Light, after His own image. (Eph. 4:24) True, sometimes, transcendent sleep is not so sweet; sometimes, these holy dreams are terrifying. All the more reason to pay attention. Those dreams may mean the soul needs our care and feeding.

Dreams that teach, correct, and even heal are not from "below." And praying in the Spirit before sleep (praying *into* sleep) may invite the sweet dreams that speak of holiness. For why would the Holy Spirit grace us only when the sun is out?

———

CHAPTER 3

Transcendent Dreams

For in him we live, and move, and have our being...
For we are also his offspring.
(ACTS 17:28)

WHEN A CERTAIN man retired, he felt something was amiss. For months, he struggled with the sense that his working life had just begun—that there was much more to do in his chosen field. But what? How? One night, a dream "tone" brought an answer: In the morning he awoke refreshed, energized, certain of his next professional steps. He did not recall even one fragment of his dream, but the interactive mood of it led him. He knew what he wanted to do. An unusual peace lingered. For the rest of his life, when directions fogged up, he drew on the clarity of that experience.

Sometimes, not the particular symbols or story lines of holy dreams haunt us, but feelings, the aftermath or sense of things, *the way these dreams transmit* the depths and heights of consciousness from whence they come. Holy dreams carry eternal messages.

Aren't there certain nights—remarkable nights—when, during sleep we somehow sense some good, some Light all about us? (Ps. 139:11)

Oswald Chambers explains the idea. Though he wasn't speaking of dreams, he insists that *we must work out what God works in.*[21]

Rather than limiting the Divine to this or that hour, corner of church, or wilderness walk, like the man above who profited from just a sliver of insight, let's mull over any whisper of guidance that the Holy Spirit brings to the spirit of our mind.[22] Let's work out what God works in.

We frequently hear reports from people whose family members have passed on, who are comforted during a dream about their loved one's eternal well-being. Not only the saints or mystics experience that sort of sleep.[23]

One woman reported, "After my mother passed away, I was grief-stricken. Then, in a dream, I saw her sitting calmly beside me in a chair looking happy, wordlessly saying, 'Be well, be glad—everything is fine.'"

---

21 Oswald Chambers, *op cit*

22 Oswald Chambers, *op cit*, 158.

23 I've often heard a familiar refrain on late night talk-radio. Callers tell of similar dreams, wherein a deceased loved one appears, usually at the foot of the bed, and reports, often telepathically, that he or she is fine, and to be happy.

In my opinion, that example is not necessarily a *holy* dream. It is far too personal, too commonly experienced. However, depending on the message one discerns, it could be. Moreover, it is a solid sample of reassurance, perhaps inspiration, gained during an elevated time of sleep.   At such times, in the spirit of our mind, we are consoled. (A variation of that dream-pattern returns later.)

One Critical Condition

Can we *accept* the idea from the Book of Daniel that, correctly interpreted, the uncommon dream can be prophetic? Not only are some holy dreams predictive, and as such puncture life's illusory and ultra-materialistic bubble, but also these tend to further spiritual wholeness. Holiness is not an all or nothing condition. We are tending toward it, ever growing. There are stops and starts, regressions, advances along the way. A dream that feels significant can keep us on the straight and narrow, particularly when our road seems too steep, and we feel too weak to carry on.

Again St. John Bosco guides us: one critical condition of holy dreams is this: Natural dreams are of the flesh, and do *not* conform to the dreams of holiness. We could say, natural dreams are of the carnal mind, the bodily senses—some very useful, very necessary, but of the earthly nonetheless.

The holy dream raises awareness, lifts the mind into the Transcendent.

Also, natural dreams are plentiful. The holy dream is infrequent, intense, haunting.

It guides us, may reveal our next *spiritual* steps. In these dreams, we can ask—and often can "hear" answered—what to do in challenging circumstances. Frequently, our answers come much later.

If we feel *called* to develop our spiritual intelligence— intuition, wisdom, reason—not merely seek out lofty theories, it follows that we are meant to discern the difference between…

(a) the rare dream in which God "speaks," and
(b) those most usual times, when dreams just could result from an undigested pizza.

Skillfully facilitated dialogue on such matters, for instance conversations with our most trusted, qualified, spiritual elders and/or companions, can deepen understandings. What, for example, is the difference between a psychologically clarifying dream and a holy dream? A Bible study group might use this question as a good discussion point. My suggestions follow shortly. First, day or night, one principle can guide us.

One Enduring Rule

A certainty exists for a life of genuine worship: God increases progressively *with* us—*within* us—with or without our help. The rule is that *Love increases itself,* " for the building up of itself in love." (Eph. 4:16)   Awake or asleep, whether as a still, small voice or as a brilliant, overpowering "light from heaven," God brings us to our knees (Acts 9:3–6). Whether we seek the Lord or are utterly uncaring, God chooses the time and place for speaking into our hearts. And all the more *if we listen; if we hearken diligently,* spiritually, to whatever's going on. The spiritual dimension is unlike the material. It's unseen. We must engage our spiritual senses—not the physical senses. But how? Sadly, the Spirit is not obligated, psychologically speaking, to be logical, not always prompting our most "well adjusted" choices. That's a bitter pill to swallow for those of us who need to stay in control of everything. (Which is nearly everyone.)

My mother told me she once refused to board an airplane for no earthly reason. She and my father were headed for Asia, but she wouldn't budge from her seat in the waiting area. My dad, an urbane intellectual, was furious. They missed their flight. The plane took off. And skidded off the runway in a crash. How do we explain the cues we get from our inner realms? How do we heed these with wisdom? If God guides and we choose; if we are acutely aware, listening inwardly, aren't we often called foolish? With that tag, aren't there resemblances between the very creative and those with a religious and/or spiritual inclination?

In our usual mind we are living in sense-based, sensual, self-centered states-- as if sleepwalkers, unaware of the Divine with and all around us. *That* Love fills every nanoparticle of space to meet us where we are.

The illogical nature of dreams applies here. We have noted a thin membrane between a psychologically clarifying dream and a holy one.[24]

The following could illustrate the difference, yet shows Love's workings...

An elderly person felt bereft at Christmas when his home—empty of family and friends—was also devoid of holiday feeling. There were no gifts, no celebrations of the Season. One night during that period he dreamt he'd bought himself a host of things he'd wanted: Inexpensive luxuries—garden tools, a new book, a new cell phone—but festively wrapped nonetheless. His rooms were now glittering with red, green, and gold-colored packages, tied with silver and golden bows and happy little silver bells. Now, his dining table was overcrowded with bright, cheery presents—all for him. He woke up happy, thinking, "Well, there's no reason I can't be good to myself even if my children don't

---

24 Naturally, these can overlap. For now, it seems helpful to make a distinction.

visit and my wife is gone." His dream comforted him and led to a practical change in choice and attitude. That's Love, working.

By contrast, consider a classic tale: A widow, still angry at her dead husband for some transgression, had a dream about him. In it, he was in heaven, surrounded by blissfully joyous friends and family. Yet, he looked forlorn. His friends asked him, "Why are you sad? All worries are over now." To which he replied, "I know my wife is still angry with me and so I am sad that she hasn't forgiven me. Now it's too late for me to do anything about it. I am so sorry."

The widow awoke, weeping. Aloud, she cried, "Dear one, I forgive you. I forgive you. Please be joyful and rest in peace. I love you forever."[25]

The first example is a psychologically clarifying dream: That man realized the only thing stopping him from enjoying the holidays was himself. His dream relates to daily life. He abruptly improved an attitude that a good therapist probably would help him address, perhaps more gradually.

The second example relates to eternity and to spiritually received virtues, like forgiveness, the God kind of love that transcends time and the grave. That love is beyond "self" alone. It opens the heart and endures forever. Love that increases Itself is in both dreams, in different ways.

---

25 Martin Buber, *Tales from the Hasidim, Book II* (New York: Schocken Books, 1947).

A healthy, well-balanced individual uses all relevant dreams to grow more integrated. A spiritually minded individual, if graced with a holy dream, also is guided into a high degree of the Love and "Light that is our Life." (John 1:4) *That* Love, *that* Light blesses self-*and*-other.

For Your Consideration

The words, the stories, the symbols, the very tone of transcendent sleep restore the soul. And can lavish on her any and all of the values, virtues, and instructions of Kingdom citizenship. To incline ourselves to such potentials is to gain the treasures of Heaven. That involves a progressive unfolding, a praise-filled heart—the praise so needed to glorify God's grace, which is already bestowed on us, in the Beloved. (See Eph. 1:5–8)

With its uncommon dreams, transcendent sleep can seem like a prayer. Not that sleep *is* prayer precisely, but that as the Carmelite author Augustine Ichiro Okumura suggests, there are times when we "sleep in God," times when we sleep in total peace, trust, and abandonment. This, to me, is that sweet sleep, when we awaken "in God and accomplish God's will."[26]

---

26 Augustine Ichiro Okumura, OCD, *Awakening to Prayer* (ICS Publications, 1994), 33.

Our Ongoing Framework

For the Mighty One has done great things for me;
And holy is His name.
(Luke 1:49)

WHEN SOLOMON WAS young, God appeared to him in a dream. He said to the lad, "Ask what you will, and I will give thee." (1 Kings 3:5) Solomon had always loved the Lord. Even in youth he had turned his mind and heart heavenward. Instead of riches and power or glory he simply asked for discernment—wisdom's ability to judge righteously—and he asked for an understanding heart.

Here is our ongoing living or evolving framework: The holy dream helps us live uncomplicatedly in an *atmosphere* of loving God above all things, and loving God's creatures as ourselves. That pure and innocent love, its climate of consciousness takes care of us—day and night. It does no good to wish for a holy dream, to seek the ten steps or "how to" of the matter as if God were our personal ATM machine.

Solomon's predisposition toward goodness is God-given—a sign of the spiritual wholeness that comes from God. That goodness starts with God. It elevates us—in the spirit of our mind—in all of life, which includes sleep.

Since only God is holy, our holiest themes in dreams reflect God's presence. I surmise that David, Joseph, Jacob, and Solomon were *preoccupied* by the things of God. Here, too, a singular focus is an essential quality of both the creative mind and those with a religious call.

With What—or Whom—Are We Preoccupied?

Earlier we noted that dreams of every sort strike a common, collective chord of recognition. Since everyone—all of humankind—has an inner life, as the great psychoanalyst (to me, a probable mystic) Carl Jung pointed out, dreams reflect the goings-on within us—conscious or otherwise. If we ignore the things of heaven, our prayer will not become an intimate *relationship* with a living God. Then our prayer is hollow.

Furthermore, holy dreams—unlike natural ones—provide quiet, sacred prompts. Not all dreams stimulate holy motivations. A dream can prompt us to wake up in the middle of the night, get up, and devour an entire apple pie – topped with a pint of Ben & Jerry's Chunky Monkey ice cream. Triggers goad us day and night to all sorts of acts. Perhaps a reasonable spiritual discipline is to stay conscious of our provocative thoughts, and to practice distinguishing between our toxic and helpful thoughts. So comes awareness of our inner life, and with that might arrive the true learning that helps us grow whole.

As with Solomon's holy dream, our own can seem profound. Some function much like a parable with a moral; if skillfully, responsibly interpreted and understood, that can guide us *and* benefit others through us.

For those tending toward spiritual wholeness, God and man somehow work together. We see this *all* through the Bible, where—dream or no dream—common fishermen, householders, even prostitutes ("ordinary" people like us) display heroic virtue just by receiving and acting on God's word. That courage and intuitive responsiveness, however, has little to do with *personal* perfection.

Self-Perfection as Vanity

It pleases our inner adversary to watch us puff up with pride over our own piety. We brag to our friends about our prophetic dream, or smugly announce "I've learned to stop boasting!" The Lord never looks to so-called perfect people to advance

His plans. Instead, God uses the fool on the hill or an outlaw or someone eating locusts in the desert. Study the foibles of the prophets, perhaps with your Bible study group: Notice how socially inept or imperfect they were. Prophets hid in caves, resided alone in the wilderness, or while the sun blazed in a cloudless sky, built giant wooden arks for a future flood. God doesn't need us to be completely "well-adjusted" to social norms in order to do great things *through* us.

Our bloated ideas of a personal holiness or some sort of private faith—and this relates to interpretation of dreams—can make us think we're destined to pursue "what flesh and blood can never bear." [27]

Not so. When God gives us a glimpse of holiness, even in a dream, it's often just to elevate our perspective. Our dark places are now safe, so that, quite naturally and wholesomely, over time our choices in, say, thought patterns, speech, work, friendships, entertainment gradually, often imperceptibly, improve. We're generally not summoned to the desert to eat bugs. Only the rare bird gets called to join a space program and zoom off to Mars.

There is often a persistence to the dreams that carry God's thoughts into the spirit of our mind. The "lost" dream

27 Chambers, *op cit,* 87. (Although Chambers is *not* writing in any way about dreams, his message is so clear, bracing and tearing down of strongholds that in my opinion it applies to all of life.)

is a type that seems to cross the psychological-spiritual bar-
rier. In that theme, we dream that we have lost our wallet, or
our way, or can't locate someone or something. In fact, this
could be a cry from the soul when she knows she's on the
wrong track and senses danger due to errors in judgment.
Not that one knows immediately what such dreams mean,
and not that one should get all prideful about some exalted
idea. One could just notice a persistent tone or truism in
one's dreams.

When Jesus said, "I do nothing of myself..." wasn't he
saying, in part, that what he apprehended as God's will, he
carried out. Surely, there are countless ways to detect such
directives.[28]

The Self-Delusion Trap

Our job is to keep our eye on the Lord, not on ourselves. In
this, the holy ones everywhere discipline themselves to look
up, heavenward. An editor and friend tells me the Greek
word for "holy" is *hagios*, literally meaning "away from the
earth or ground." That also could mean away from the
dust-to-dust self.

---

28 See John 8:28 for only one of these utterances.

In the holiness setup, each of us is potentially rich with the attributes of the Divine. For, in essence, we creatures exist for the manifestation of God's glory—through *His* holiness. God's great secret, someone once wrote, is that He gives us Himself in a way we can never express.[29] In an inexplicable fashion, we then try to serve with whatever means we have.

More: Our holiness consists of adhering to, and loving, God as He knows Himself. That motive with its loyalty frees us from cultural programming. Somehow, that love also lets us continually die to our small, egoistical self, to be reborn into the Son's eternal Being. The small death and rebirth arrives through *intimacy of relationship* in prayer, meditation, contemplation, and—yes— that "small death" also amplifies receptivity to our inner life. Receptivity is progressive. There's always more to discover.

We come to a point in all this where, without trivializing the phrase, our whole life is prayer: The bird's song is prayer, the thought of our child, spouse or friend is prayer, the sun warm on our face is prayer.

And yet, this communion is so practical, so necessary for paying bills and cleaning cupboards, and having energy to

---

29 I *think* it was Thomas Merton, but can't say in what book or recording. Some ides of his one simply remembers.

wake up at dawn to go to work. A classic Hasidic tale explains (and I condense it greatly):

A certain rabbi taught his students that holiness is rooted in daily life. He explained the need to stay grounded in practice and tangible progress of spirituality: "It's as if God says to us, 'You shall be holy unto Me, but as humans... humanly holy unto Me.'"[30]

He seemed to say, "Let's keep it real—let's keep our feet on the ground. Ours is, after all, an *earthly* experience."

When & How?

It is perhaps a self-defeating snare to presume every memorable dream is "holy." In part, that could explain this book's encouragement of dialogue with trusted, *qualified* professionals: Like the rabbi in the last story, such professionals can help us keep our feet on the ground. It can be a relief to consult a chaplain, pastor, priest, rabbi, a family member or friend, a church or synagogue group studying the subject of dreams. Also, let's remember how helpful it may be to record selected dreams in a journal; that, too, could support our explorations and increase the power, health, and development of our inner life. All that to say, there are multiple routes to gaining understanding.

---

30 Martin Buber, *op cit* (paraphrased).

Notice a universal theme of an earlier dream in the next example. (The sample is a composite of many such reports I've heard.)

On late-night radio call-in shows, people habitually describe being greatly consoled by a distinctive type of dream. Some call these "grief dreams," others refer to them as "visitation dreams." The dreamers echo each other:

> *Shortly after my mother died—and we had been close—she appeared in a dream, standing by my bed, looking peaceful, and very young. She sort of projected the thought that she was well and that I shouldn't be sad; that we'd see each other again, one day. She uttered not one word, but I felt so reassured when I awoke.*[31]

> *How wonderful that my minister is also a confidant with whom I can discuss such ethereal matters.*

Of course, saints and the everyday saintly can experience such dreams. My impression is that saints typically have visitation dreams in which they "meet" Jesus, their favorite saint, or, say, the Virgin Mary. Saints probably know the sorts of dreams we all do. They are human. Yes, they face their mortal issues: conflicts with family, friends, and authority figures; battles of will and conscience; illness, depression. Yes,

---

31 On October 6, 2016, on *Coast to Coast AM* radio, another similar report cane from a woman who said that her deceased mother had visited her in a dream, looking young, *and* that around the same time, a relative dreamt about the caller's mother who again looked good and very young. In the relative's dream, the mother left a message with the relative, for her daughter, On October 11, 2016, a doctoral candidate researching "grief dreams" answered questions from callers about that. (One probably can hear both shows and all callers on the show's archive. (www.coasttocoastam.com)

high-minded, super-intelligent creative sorts have problems. Who doesn't?

There was turbulence between St. Francis of Assisi and his father. To many, St. Thomas of Aquinas seemed slow, and antisocial. St. Catherine of Genoa anguished about close associates. Not just saints, but *all* of us understand such things, and perhaps the more creative we are the more we get it.

In sleep, everyone's physical body—and their surroundings—influence a dream's images: Barking dogs, loud radios or TV sounds morph into dream words, plots, figures. However, we are discussing holiness, so it must and can be said that these dreams generally transcend natural influences

Spiritual Intelligence in Sleep

Some spiritual helpers—pastors, priests, academics, counselors—could care little about dreams, know even less and may discount a dream's spiritual worth. One of my good metaphysical friends mocks my idea of holy dreams, insisting that all human life—including dreams—is the illusion of the carnal mind, and should be ignored. I believe otherwise.

Why else would Scripture provide story after story of prophetic dreams? As noted, dreams take us into a different dimension of reality from which can flow wisdom.

The stress, upsets, and struggles of daily experience surface predictably in our dreams. Already mentioned are dreams of loss (e.g., sagas of lost cars, lost keys, lost teeth, lost directions, and being lost) and terrifying dreams of drowning, plane crashes, falling, or being chased; or letdowns (such as failing exams). All these are standard fare for most of us.

I believe there's much creative intricacy to sleep itself, and therefore to dreams. Christians with a religious call—or as is often said, "religious impulse"—are frequently so identified with the Lord that, at minimum, a few dreams and certainly a series of dreams can convey an inspired Godly idea, instruction, or vocation. (The latter being common, especially to the religious.) Even so, some insist that all that is merely a projection; and also the usual religious mind will incline itself to "testing the spirit" of everything.

Have We Tested "the spirits"?[32]

In one of his televised lectures, that invigorating thinker, Father John Corapi, noted that most dreams are the product of our human imagination.[33]

---

32 When it involves our *human spirit*, the word *spirits* means our sentient element; character of thought, moral nature, dominant influence, etc., in contrast to the Holy Spirit.
33 The lecture in question was on EWTN-TV, possibly in 2010. (I also may have seen it on YouTube.)

Nevertheless, he also seemed convinced that "once in a while" God (or the devil) can speak to us in a dream. For instance—if I understood correctly—during a prolonged disheartening season, one of Corapi's dreams was hilarious. Cartoon-like images buoyed up the priest, causing him to laugh so hard (while sleeping) that he woke himself up; his sides ached from laughing. Much like the aforementioned retired man, for a time he felt lighter, better, cheered up. As his remarks suggest, Corapi also apparently never forgot the experience.

For You Consideration: Testing "the spirits"

One way to test the spirit of our dreams is to discern God's character in its content; we can evaluate the symbols or words within the spiritual context of dreams. Also, the joy, peace, conviction, the sheer gladness that a dream produces in us can help that discernment. When we awaken in a hopeful, more integrated state, when faith is restored, when we've fallen asleep fearful or confused along some practical or moral line, and wake up calmer or clearer, we may well have slept "in God." In summary: I sense there are ways to tell when our attention has been drawn up to some righteous state during sleep. Nevertheless, it's prudent to tread with caution before following a dream's message.

For more—and essential—"testing" of spirits: Examine satan's character! Would he buoy up our hope or send dreams that strengthen faith, goodness, a love of beauty, life, God and neighbor? When a dream's lovely landscapes or its aftermath of strengthened virtue linger, it is not likely to be of our adversary; when we're guided toward better use of our time and talents and creative or agape love, this is our Friend. But, do we, *can* we, recognize—*receive*—the sheer poetry of grace by which light dispels the darkness? (See Gal. 5:22)

Preparation as Prayer and "Invitation": Three Ideas

Apart from what has been suggested thus far, there seem ways to "invite" helpful, perhaps also holy, dreams: Consider *preparation* as a prayer and an invitation for what we want—in this case, a holy dream or at least a hopeful, solution-oriented one.

With both spiritual and material matters, we can prepare our heart, our mind, our intention. For instance...

1. Prior to sleep, we might prepare our heart—not just with ritualized prayers, but by pulling down

"strongholds," those false gods we worship (i.e., in the day; worries; anxieties, frustrations, etc.).[34]

2. To prepare our mind, we can positively anticipate our recall of our dreams by keeping paper and pen or pencil by the bed. Highly creative people—artists, actors, poets, entrepreneurs, inventors, (whatever their formal occupation or role in life)—are well known for hyper-acuity to colors, words, and scenes of a dream. They write down ideas, day and night, on all manner of scraps: paper napkins, envelopes, invoices, desk tops, walls, even money! Ideas, like lottery tickets, are precious; even those that prove worthless need to be saved until we're ready to test their value.

3. We can *intend* to have our answer to this or that concern by either asking God in a pre-sleep prayer for our solution, or writing out a question about the issue right before sleep or visualizing the solution to a matter in some meditative fashion. Such methods are not formulas, and completely individualized.

While writing this book I heard about a person who visualized—concretized—in mental images an answer to his seeming lack of funds. Before sleep, he imagined he put his

---

34 1 Samuel 7:3 speaks about preparing our hearts—although *not* necessarily related to sleep.

checkbook and thus, to him, his dilemma into a bright red balloon and sent it away into the firmament (i.e., clouds) of his mind. He then deliberately "saw" a green balloon returning, filled with cash. He did this sort of thing nightly. One supposes in time his cash flow problem was solved. Conceivably similar practices could be done with spiritual issues.[35]

In essence, as that frugal housekeeper learned, the rule is whatever we attend to grows stronger in our lives. Attending to something—focusing on it; *being* engrossed with the matter—is a form of invitation to more of the same, deeper of the same. Attend to a problem: more potential problem. Attend to solutions, more potential solutions.

Paying attention to possibilities seems one form of service, a vital choice. Paying attention to those we love is service. For example, we have a choice between letting our cell phone ring (or turning the ringer off) when dining with family or friends, or choosing to talk to our caller and ignoring those around us. The holy dream can guide us to choose *this* day whom we will serve. (Josh. 24:15)

---

35   I am not a fan of guided visualization, but when reading Scripture, it's like poetry: my mind automatically visualizes a great deal more than the text describes. The best book I've read on that issue of the Bible as image-rich poetry is by William P. Brown, *Seeing the Psalms* (Westminster John Knox Press. London, 2002).

Part II

In a dream, in a vision of the night, when deep
sleep falleth upon man, in slumbers upon the bed;
Then he openeth the ears of men, and sealeth
their instructions.
(Job 33:15–16, KJV)

CHAPTER 5

God & Psyche

For with thee is the fountain of life;
in thy light we shall see light.
(PSALM 36:9)

AN ARTIST FELL on hard times and was forced to buy a run-down home in an equally run-down area. He entered a period of dark depression. He thought his life was over. His artistic nature abhorred the shabby rooms, lack of garden space, and graceless neighborhood. One night after weeks of torment he dreamt he occupied bright white rooms, spacious and clean. Outside, his tiny patio seemed luminous with huge red roses in cobalt pots. It was as if his space was a happy warm light in a cold, drab area.

He awoke encouraged. He realized that he could transform his home inexpensively, could create a radiant secret garden where now only weeds flourished. The current grime mirrored his pre-dream, inner landscape. That had changed.

"Why not," he wondered, "*be* light, and create light where now there is darkness?" Call that a healing or a transformation. The improvement happened within his psyche, his inmost sensibility.

The term *psyche*—or deeper mind—is accepted by most people. As noted at the outset of this book, we call these capacities by many names.

Despite that, some reject the whole notion of the unconscious. "Inner life" might then cover it all. One thing is sure: the highly gifted *creative* psyche and the highly gifted *religious* psyche are much alike in subjective richness and intensity of ardor for their calling, whether that's painting murals or saving souls— it's truly adoration. All who possess that trait need high quality, perhaps inordinate amounts, of rest and renewal.

A friend who writes cookbooks is a master home-chef. She once told me, " After finishing a project, I take to my couch for weeks." (Our own gambit could be to watch *Netflix.) Rest, renewal and an enriched psyche are related.*

That topic and more we shall gradually revisit. First, why has so little been said of that similarity between the religious and creative psyche? Moreover, do we, as a culture, unwisely celebrate filmmakers or artists, no matter how dull or crass their art, but dismiss the religious, no matter how vibrant their influence? Is it only the rare family that encourages children to enter a ministry, while the norm seems that most families applaud their children's athletic or law school ambitions? These familial responses affect a child's psyche.

"Psyche" suggests the *entirety* of our mental composition, which some define as the soul, the spirit, even the breath.[36] Whatever our vocabulary, it does seem that once our inner land is an adornment to us—a *source* of beauty, fertility, skillful means, and a degree of interior harmony—things in our outer world probably conform. Not always, and not instantly. Such flourishing could take years. Of course, these qualities are of God, Pure Being, Source. And much of that creative, interior soil gets tilled and nourished during R.E.M. (i.e., rapid eye movement) or dream sleep.

Jungian author and minister John Sanford writes that there is "… an essential identity between the God-image in the final order of the universe, or the transcendent God" *and* ourselves.[37] For nearly everyone, that "God-image" unfolds gradually in the psyche. Here, within the psyche, lives the glory and grandeur of the Lord, unseen, humble, much overlooked, no doubt crucified daily.

With Him" the fruit of the earth" will be a pride and adornment. (Is. 4:2) In a real and substantive sense, we are created

---

36 *New Webster's Dictionary of the English Language* (New York: Delaire Pub., 1981),1205.
37 John Sanford, *Dreams: God's Forgotten Language* (San Francisco, CA., HarpersSan-Francisco, 1989), 182. (For emphasis, the italics are mine.)

to *be* that original Garden where everything flourishes and is "very good." (Gen.1:30)

Consider the infinite routes by which God's glorious Image works into our psyche. Both despair and jubilation can make us more receptive. At all hours (if we're aware), a heightened inner senses can surface and, as with the artist above, that can bring healing. In prayer or meditation, while raking leaves or changing a tire, one sometimes is flooded with fresh, sublimely useful ideas. What we focus on in the day, persists.

One night, at six years old, a friend who was already full of religious sensibility dreamt that Jesus stood near her bedside, beckoning her to live only for him. In young adulthood, she joined a monastery where she's lived ever since. With proper support, a child's psyche can blossom early.

Isn't openness to our inner workings basic for creative, spiritual sorts? Unfortunately, more rigid types discount the import of even unforgettable dreams. To their own detriment, I say.

Are we Westerners schooled away from God's "glorious Branch" with us? Have we *learned* to ignore the language of dreams?

Author Huston Smith tells us that, traditionally, Eastern cultures—e.g., India—have long honored the divine potentials of dreams. Yogis remain acutely aware—awake—in sleep. The great ones insist that even in dreamless sleep they typically are more intensely mindful than in waking consciousness.[38]   That tradition is ours, too. When did we in the West pour subjective cement over our psyche?[39]

Poets and painters, musicians and mystics of every culture live out what psychiatrist A. Reza Arasteh has termed "final integration"—to him, rebirth in the Cosmic Self; to me, rebirth in the new man or risen Christ; for others, who can say?[40]

Given Carl Jung's influence, these days many non-Jungians have high regard for dream analysis. Jung's original thought, his ideas of a collective unconscious, introversion and extraversion, and the concept of the archetype have wide impact on almost everyone—including the general public, spiritual directors and clerics of many religious

---

38 Huston Smith, *Cleansing the Doors of Perception* (New York: Jeremy P. Tarcher/Putnam, 1970).

39 One reads of indigenous people training children to be active witnesses (lucid) in their dreams (e.g., to *consciously* turn in dreams, to face—not run from—their dream adversaries). In the Amazon, certain tribes are said to use plant hallucinogens (to smoke or as teas) to enhance spiritual experiences. One such plant (*Ayehuasca*) releases DMT, the *same compound* released in sleep by the pineal gland (aka "the third eye"), which also produces other substances that stimulate dreams (e.g., serotonin, melatonin, etc.) especially during deep REM (rapid eye movement) sleep.
How intriguing that prayer, meditation, yoga, probably some types of chanting, and even certain high-stress situations—e.g., near-death, extreme trauma, etc.—"move" the brain *beyond* its customary programming (normal mental "chatter" stops) and mind transcends brain. In all such cases, the pineal gland naturally releases its various compounds that enhance dreams, hallucinations, etc.

40 A. Reza Arasteh, *Final Integration* (Institute of Perspective Analysis). (No publication date or location was provided.)

backgrounds. Jung's thought-leadership is unquestioned. One example that we can use: Jung encouraged his patients to pay special attention to the dream series. Good advice for many reasons.

About the Dream Series

For highly creative, spiritual (or religious) types, the dream series—a chain of dreams with a single idea or message—tends to involve a "cross." That could be a move into some unknown, a sacrifice or turn away from something low, unattractive, dark—a habitual thought pattern of fear or narcissism, a lack of caring about others, or one of the seven deadly sins. We work out the better way in a dream series if and as we are willing to bear it. As we live out the "essential Image"—the glorious, beautiful instruction or message that God has worked in—the dream series either stops or changes. After which, we may start to be that good ground that bears good fruit.

Consider These Examples

One individual had a string of dreams featuring cats and kittens. Her dream series continued, and evolved over about two decades.

Initially, the animals in her dreams were lost, alone, neglected, very thirsty. In these first dreams, the dreamer was always upset, frantic, hunting about for clean water and clean water dishes, not knowing how else to help, feeling helpless. Typically, she woke up crying, feeling she was meant to care for *all* creatures, but how? She kept remembering Christ's words when on the cross, "I thirst," and she was heartsick. Over time, she realized it was her soul that was crying, abused, neglected, *thirsty*.

That dream series persisted for years, each one influencing her everyday attitudes, helping her yield incrementally to her true vision and vocation of what Life was asking of her. That growth illustrates the *true* learning discussed earlier. It starts within, even while outer resources—other people, books, experiences, etc.—are critical to such growth. We were not created for the world, as I believe St. Augustine taught: The world is made for us—for the soul's growth, for instance, in her capacity to love. Here again, more true learning. For the question of how we're each called to love rightly usually is answered by beyond-classroom lessons.

With that spirit of discovery burning within her, that dreamer sought roles by which to help herself and others, *in her own way.* That is key.

Authentic individuals feel pressed to be themselves: which means unique. As a result, each in his or her fashion, longs to design a meaningful life. Which takes creativity. Not all succeed. In the spiritual, unseen components of life, doing our utmost to be true to ourselves counts.

We often see that bid for authenticity as naturalness or as spontaneity in the very young, sometimes in the very old. Every truly genuine person is somehow just being themselves, flaws and foibles included. Thus they can be considered a bit of an odd duck. If we're honest, we 'll see some oddness in ourselves, especially if we dream lavishly —for dreams unearth our truths.

Spiritual wholeness involves the type of person we *are*— the type of life we are called to live. Hermits and statesmen; potters, pianists, and householders: all are summoned to wholeness, *each in his or her own way.*[41] That dreamer of cats and kittens ultimately decided, "I wanted to contribute, to express regard for others, yet needed to be more than a token 'do-gooder'— I sought authentic service, or I'd end up 'thirsty' myself." Answers came slowly and required innovation.

Just as dreamers learn that dream elements relate to one's own psyche, so that woman determined a first task was

---

41 That drive for wholeness and authenticity, when thwarted easily distorts us, goes underground, converts to mental illness, hostility, depression, addictions, and more. Healthy inner drives, if snuffed out, "quenched," transmute into unhealthy emotions, choices, anger, sorrow, etc. So comes the 'gnashing of teeth…'. Or so I believe.

to bring pure, fresh water (figuratively speaking) to her own life.[42]

Since she worked in a compelling, but intensely competitive, environment, she was surrounded by smart, aggressive associates. They were her friends. She cared for them To her, her dreams' cats and kittens represented a more innocent aspect of self-and-other. Each time the dream returned, she understood more: *Everyone* needed living water.

After rearranging her working life, she composed things for a real calling. "To me," that dreamer noted, "this was like positioning flowers in a bouquet– a hobby of mine. One element must enhance the other. That aesthetic now seems *my* art of life." She formed new like-minded friendships. She adjusted her schedule to allow time for religious involvements. Then the dream series changed.

Soon, the animals always had clean bowls of fresh water. The dream animals looked contented, properly cared for. Finally, as she embraced her own, more innocent nature and call, the dream series stopped altogether. Intriguingly, the lives of saints and the saintly reveal similar, probably universal patterns, as shown by the next example.

---

42 See John 4:10, Eph. 1:13,14: For believer, and the idea is mention in the Old Testament (aka: Hebrew Bible) and the New Testament ,"living water," is that flowing of the Holy Spirit in and out of hearts redeemed by God.

One Saint's Leadership

We find shared motifs of holy dreams in talented people—creative types and — yes— the religiously gifted. (These are frequently, as mentioned, one and the same, but not always.) The saint and the saintly, for example, are — to me —as exceptional in their own rights as the physicist, the painter, the inventor of the internet. Take St. John Bosco: In his biography, we read of his talent for dreaming, dream interpretation, and influence — leadership. The themes of his dreams would seem to tap into a deep collective imperative: To love.

One of Bosco's dream series is reminiscent of the earlier set. These two dream series are more than one hundred years apart, and have little to do with the dreamers' cultures or their life-contexts. The first dreamer is a modern woman in business; the next, a 19th Century working priest, later a Saint.

As a boy, Bosco repeatedly dreamt of needy animals: Goats, dogs, cats, and others, both tame and wild. A Lady (the Virgin Mary) appeared often in his dreams, telling him to strengthen and humble himself, and to prepare to care for her children as if he were caring for animals that he loved. In sleep, he looked back at the animals and saw the wild ones had turned into gentle lambs. Then, still asleep, he began to cry; he didn't understand what this meant. The

Lady comforted him, placed her hand on his head, and said, "In due time, everything will be clear."

John Bosco had that dream series for about eighteen years. Each time, he envisioned a life's work more clearly, saw future obstacles, saw how to overcome them.[43]   So profound were dreams as a source of inspiration for Bosco that he circulated descriptions of them to his followers.

How might we discern God's message in the spirit of our holiest dreams? Don't we need some sort of sensitizing practice? Praying and meditating over the dream's content itself, contemplatively studying its poetic, artistic or spiritual hues, particularly in repeating dreams, recording our notes in a journal, engaging in dialogue with a trusted helper—might all be useful. Understanding a holy dream is art, not science – a cookie-cutter approach probably won't reveal much of the deep things of life.

This and more is intuitive "art". It can deepen comprehension of the eternal instructions revealed to us, using Job's words, as we "slumber upon the bed" in transcendent nights.

------

43 *Forty Dreams of St. John Bosco* (Tan Books and Publishers, 1996), 5.

CHAPTER 6

The Meaning is the Message

Do not interpretations belong to God?
(GENESIS 40:8)

WE SAW IN the last chapter, that the depressed artist's dream of a lovely living space cheered him up. He awoke full of hope. However, before he could improve his life concretely, he had to understand how his dream related to the context of each day. That involved paying attention to the dream's elements, pondering its story, *receiving* its Light. For him, the meaning, that a lovely, airy home need not be opulent, *was* the message: He could improve his lot in life right now; he could choose to live beautifully—even in low rent rooms.

So, too, as we patiently reflect on daily life to assess current situations in relation to our dream's meanings— or "message"—we tend to become clearer. No matter how amorphous or mystical our holy dream may seem, its meanings aim to be *known*. I suspect we often create or make our meanings—fill in the blanks, as it were—according to our level of wisdom.

"Every night these days," explained one entrepreneur, " I dream about rough roads and bridges. Common sense tells me there's no big existential message here. I'm planning to move, don't want to, and those images mean to me there's a winding, perhaps arduous crossing I'll face if I don't change my attitude. Here's my message: You get out of things what you put in: I need to give this move my all."

Ben Shahn, that amazingly gifted graphic artist and, through his art, social activist, noted that we all have a one-of-a-kind inner landscape. Which, when well tended and well expressed, can be of unceasing wonder to others. To be and express who we intuit we are at our ground of being, is to be of service, both to ourselves *and* to our world. The holy dream is meant to advance that service.

No doubt, imagination, maturity and emotional balance help in deciphering our "inner landscape." That trio of traits may explain my support of *qualified* professional dialogue. Sometimes two minds are better than one. Also, it can help to hear ourselves speak out our truths and hear those reflected back to us by a caring, level-headed other.

In ancient times, it was considered a mark of humility to ask a spiritual elder for opinions. In our day, we may pride ourselves on toughing it out, going it alone. An old desert father cautioned a younger one against that: "They who listen to a spiritual parent can often profit more than those who move off to live in a cave." [44]

A two-way conversation is regularly dynamic, energetic and requires lively attention be put forth by each one. That takes energy, concentration, caring. *Hearing* someone's deepest heart is an act of love. Few of us in our distracted era manage that well. Understanding anything worthwhile is no passive activity.

Which is one reason the contemplative arts are so *mentally* engrossing. You may think meditators just sit around gazing at their navels. Some say of the religious, "They're so heavenly minded, they're no earthly good." (Would we describe reflective sorts like a Billy Graham, a Nelson Mandela, a Bishop Desmond Tutu or a Gandhi as "no earthly good"?) Inwardly, when listening or praying much is happening. These are energetic pursuits.

Quilters, sculptors, carpenters, and chess players must know that same contemplative mind. It takes mental energy to meditate effectively on anything, even work tasks. What's not so well known is that effective prayer and meditation, in

---

44 Sister Benedicta, SLG, *Wisdom of the Desert Fathers* (Fairoaks, Oxford. SLG Press, 1998), 49. Paraphrased.

the long run, boost mental energy. That's especially true for we who are harkening to the ineffable Word within.

Both the Old and New Testaments teach us that God's voice and angel messengers are present with us day and night. Yet, we must scrutinize, then develop, our innate spiritual abilities. That's part of the aforementioned intuitive art.

Daniel's and Joseph's talents were sought out by kings and commoners alike. These men were gifted in an inborn way. *Our* gifts are also inborn, but usually require drawing out, education, development. And, yes, the work we feel called to do, work we generally love to do, assists in that development.

When asked to explain a dream, Joseph's question might match ours: "Do not interpretations belong to God?" Here's where contemplative prayer, meditation, and other pondering sorts of practices come in. Which need not be esoteric: pulling weeds can be mindlessly or mindfully done.

To echo a previous principle: We grow spiritually whole as we are separated unto God. It's worth repeating: That growth starts with God Who loves us first; *then* we love, turn, choose to move in faith filled directions. God "speaks"; then we hear. God illumines; then we "see." God calls; then we answer. (Hopefully.)

If we're turning toward the things of God, whether we're mulling over an investment or a dream's meanings, we'll increasingly pray first and patiently wait out our answers. Scripture study, meditation, and journal work can all contribute to that process. We'll tap into our psyche—*our deepest spiritual sensibilities*—to cultivate the skills that Joseph and Daniel had in abundance. It's like playing the piano or singing: Some people are just more gifted than others. We all have gifts. That is why we need each other variously, and is also why we consult our trustworthy spiritual elders for help in drawing out whatever talents we have to offer.

All this is part of the drill—as that old saw has it, "How do you get to the concert stage? Practice, practice, practice."

Another possibility: Instead of robotically checking with dominant others to see what they think, we may want to mull things over for ourselves, and then check with those we trust most for input on a matter. Authoritarian sorts often *need* to coax us into their too-certain or overly programmed explanations of a dream; those tending toward holiness generally pray first about all things. After which, they may (or may not) consult some reliable other for a second opinion. As a physician once told me when I debated having a serious surgery, " Trust your gut." In that context, isn't "the gut" our inmost sensibility?

The Helper's Role

Couldn't dream analysis involve a variety of approaches, each enabling the dreamer to integrate whatever shard of spiritual light is received? If we are gaining skills, first we'll be hearing God's still, small voice—not that of others. That's a kind of naiveté. Our dream samples aim to illustrate that innocence: It's to the "babes" that God unveils his hidden things. (See Mt. 11:25

Interior Hearing

There is a point in contemplative prayer when our ears "open" and we hear that ineffable Voice. That hearing is individuated, again—unique to the kind of person we are. Some people see images; others receive guidance from the Holy Spirit during the day, right after or during prayer for instance, or while shaving, showering or driving to work. A slogan on a billboard answered a prayer of a friend.

In this, one feels or senses one's way. Be assured, for the most part, we are not hearing audible voices. Generally, the gist of a dream is the message. Said one man, "My emotional state tells me about my dream." That's particularly true if we pay attention before jumping right out of bed.

One person remarked, " When I first wake up after a powerful dream, or a piece of it in mind, I stay very still. I reflect on it. *Then,* I grab my calendar, right by my bedside, and jot down a few key scenes – anything that I can remember. Maybe it's a word or two. I try to capture the essence of it, and as I'm so busy, I just get on with my to-do list. Later, fragments of the dream may return to mind. Still later, I sense the meaning – don't ask how that works. I really don't know, but I think it has something to do with intent – I'm determined to understand it."

In St. John Bosco's dreams, guides appeared *within* the dreams themselves: Angels, St. Francis de Sales, and "the Lady" spoke to him, directly in the dream. His guides echoed God's word. Bosco then successfully circulated his dreams in written form to followers (who waited for installments).

Our dreams may not include guides, and we may or may not seek out counseling to expand understanding. That's a personal call.

If we elect dialogue, whatever our collaborator's creed, a spiritual helper should be a valuable sounding board who…

- listens discerningly *first,* to hear *our* thoughts, only then offers ideas,
- points out possible spiritual patterns,
- encourages *us* to examine, articulate, advance the dream's essence,
- emphasizes the character, qualities, and nature of our "new man" so as to draw out our wisdom about

the dream's holy lessons. A holy dream will somehow reflect God's word.

The American Trappist monk, Thomas Merton, in most of his books, proposed that our new nature is exemplified by spiritual liberty—not slavery. In a practical sense that means in the Light of God our fear, anxieties, conformity to corrupting norms begin to wane. The soul finds her proper footing and her freedom from doubt, hesitation, and the wobbling of indecision. *Then* her finest future is revealed. Is that not power?

That intrinsic power comes from God as one is becoming integrated—all of a piece. Someone once said that integration involves all our little conflicting desires and values work together toward one overarching, God-given goal. For a contemplative, or one with a religious impulse, that goal is union with the Lord. Which I believe happens as one is drawn into a deep interior stillness, and, yes—solitude: the kind where, despite being in a crowd, we sense a quiet strength, and a reminder, "Greater is He that is in you than he who is in the world." (1 John 4:4) To be established in that state, to me, is to have entered the "shalom" of our life.[45]

That knowing power flows from intimacy with God. Around the world, people sense that strength, hear such

---

45 Shalom (sometimes "sholom") means peace, harmony, wholeness, completion, prosperity, tranquility and more. (see Wikipedia or any good dictionary.)

reassurances differently. Which, in part, may be why Jesus taught his followers that he had other sheep "that are not of this fold..." and also heard his voice. (John 10:16) We who are strident in our faith sometimes forget that teaching. Which also could explain why the motifs of holy dreams are universally shared. How could the Divine be confined to one group or geographic area?

In the West some call that knowing strong faith; in the East, it might be termed God-consciousness. As before, I have keen respect for your preferred language. Should you ask, "How long does that inner strength or integration take to develop?" I'd ask, "How long is a piece of string?"

Interior Hearing as Discernment

If we possess that integration, or *spiritual* wholeness, we'll notice ourselves seeking God's word and will for all things, including dreams.

From that guideline come others, especially for a dialogue. Such as...

1. The dreamer "owns" his or her dreams. Meanings are for us, want to be known. Through, say, thoughtful study of Scripture, it's likely God interprets all things. And, as dreamers, we can discern our meanings while keeping notes, studying, or collaborating with a professional.

To further dialogue we may want to first provide...

- a bit of background on the history or circumstances of life—say, the tone, thoughts or mental atmosphere of sleep surrounding the dream, and
- initial insights about the dream and its words, tone, symbols, import, etc.

2. Our pastor, spiritual counselor, or trusted friend also could ask guiding questions (but in most cases would not impose a fixed analysis).

3. As dreamers, we'll move back and forth, from the dream content to the context of our life. We'll focus on any lasting impressions of the dream—that task could continue indefinitely. If we're a qualified helper, we may prompt that inquiry by exploring things that seem...

- Relevant: What "hues" or aspects of the dream endure?
- Instructive: What seems most meaningful, intense, memorable, troublesome, joyful about the dream? Why?
- Godly: What characteristics of holiness seem to apply?

One person said, "It's fine to be tentative in such discussions. I now expect the nub of a dream to evolve gradually."

The thoughts and conditions of the dreamer's life often resurface repeatedly as he or she circles around the themes of holiness. Usually the dialogue will reveal a bit more about those concerns, values, friendships, and moral dilemmas than have been divulged before. Thus does the onion get peeled.

And also...

1. The dreamer might identify any and all repeating or memorable symbols, images, themes, conflicts, etc. Some issues repeat endlessly, even from *childhood*.

2. The dreamer, perhaps in concert with the helper, may choose to enlist the support of Scripture, wherever possible, to clarify any spiritual issues.

3. Word study: Contemplative study may play a significant role in explaining the specifics of a dream. In samples that follow we've underlined some of the words that the dreamer wants to define. This could take place over much time.

   a.) If the spiritual helper feels a need to describe certain words, these might be introduced with questions such as, "What does thus and such mean to you?" "What does the word XYZ signify to you?"

   b.) Should the dreamer spontaneously offer a spiritual dream in some group setting, the facilitator may remind group members of strict confidentiality issues.

If our professional helper is disinterested in spiritual topics, Scripturally limited or tediously cerebral (e.g., head-trip-ping; lost in bookish meanings), if he or she demands com-plex interpretation—exalted, legalistic, literal, etc.—when we, as the dreamer, prefer simpler ideas, we may withdraw, shut down, or somehow lose interest in continuing the dia-logue—all signs that the professionals are off the mark. Or, on the other hand, sometimes it is *we* who cannot bear to look at or consider what the professionals suggest. We easily balk at working out what God works in.

It's so important to be *adroitly* frank. In a dialogue, give and take is a two-way "exchange of selves" (as Thomas Merton once called it).[46]

While we as the dreamer "own" the dream, the Holy Spirit provides guidance, however subtle, to all involved in dialogue about it . Guidance comes as each one's prayer, meditation and contemplative study of, say, Scripture, lets the Holy Spirit cast His Light.

Carl Jung noted the significance of "archetypes" in the psyche—*pre-existing* forms or energies and perhaps func-tional motifs. These color, shape, and influence our life, and of course our dreams, fantasies, feelings. We could realize

---

46 Merton defined *dialogue* in that way in one of his recorded lectures on "inter-religious" dialogue. I've loved *all* of his recorded talks, available still (I believe) from the Thomas Merton Center.

that our own receptivity to the archetype (or essence) within is critical for comprehending pretty much anything, not just dreams. [47] To me, the archetype is a *seed* that, if not crushed, produces fruit *after its own kind.* (See Gen. 1:11-12)

When Is A Frog Not a Frog?

Lest anyone worry that all dream work is too cumbersome, the following story may help: Two hosts on early morning talk-radio were discussing the notion of dream interpretation. They seemed to be joking about the whole concept. Then one said something like, rather seriously to my ear, "But I had a dream last night that meant something — I'm still thinking about it today; I don't think I'll ever forget it."

He went on to describe his dream which involved a huge, pale-colored bullfrog, stalking a bird, then eating it alive. The dreamer, sounding shaken (to me), said (and I'm paraphrasing), "I can't get the picture out of my mind of that long, thin, red tongue lashing out, wrapping around that little bird and pulling it into its mouth. It was awful." After which, the two seemed to return to their light banter, while tossing about ideas and characteristics of the frog, mostly that frogs croak, that to croak, in slang, means to die and that perhaps the dream

---

47 Carl Jung, *Memories, Dreams, Reflections* (New York: Vintage Book Edition, 1985).

carried an ominous message about death. It occurred to me, as a listener, that if the two had been conversing in a more private atmosphere, their talk might well have produced a few more serious, high-quality ideas about the dream's significance. As an eavesdropper on that intriguing dialogue, I wanted to hear more; it certainly seemed as though, to that dreamer, that frog was much more than a mere frog.

Until such time as technology finds a way into our brains where, according to science fiction sagas, memories and the gist or meanings of things are stored, there may not be a quick-fix method for interpreting or even remembering most dreams. Fortunately, the more intense a dream— holy or otherwise — the more likely we'll recall important aspects; the more likely these aspects have some sort of implication for everyday life.

Do we prefer informal or more structured ways to under-stand a dream's possible message? Either way explains why con-templation is less a "seeking," for God's touch in a dream (as though He was distant and far removed) and much more a receiving the One and only Reality that is already and forever going on—*with* us. To yield to the Presence that *Is,* is a yielding that leaves interpretations to God. That, too, is prayer.

———

CHAPTER 7

Words, Symbols, Samples

Let the one who is taught the word share all good
things with him who teaches.
(GALATIANS 6:6)

A WOMAN, LONG divorced from her husband, still shared a companionable relationship with him. The two had little in common, yet lived near one another and despite their divorce, felt like family. One night the woman had the following dream:

> *I was standing near or on a highway. A white truck was driving away from me. In my dream, I heard myself calling out plaintively to my former husband, 'Don't forget me.' (I didn't see him in that truck, but knew he was in there, driving away.)*

She woke up sobbing. And for weeks after that dream, the slightest thought of it brought her to tears. Later, we use a few dream samples to discuss word and Scripture study. Although the dream above seems more psychological than spiritual, the dreamer looked up words in a bible dictionary for much clarification. Which anyone can do.

Was her dream a forewarning? Was one of them dying, moving away, growing emotionally more distant? What was the meaning of the white truck? She knew it must have held special significance, but what?

As with that dream, many pieces of the puzzle may be missing. Or, we forget some elements. If we're spiritually intelligent we'll sense what dream words, symbols, or stories have importance. Scripture can help us gain metaphorical meanings of words, even when a dream isn't really "holy."

Before looking at a few words and symbols from dream samples, a few more comments about dialogue seem in order. That, too, could lean on the study of words and symbolic images. The word-study method may not be typically employed in, say, therapy or counseling sessions. However, as mentioned earlier, so many of us in ever-widening circles of interaction, are conversing about dreams and other personal topics, the system could prove useful. Also, dreams have so many oddities, in my opinion the concreteness of defining words when in dialogue may enhance the process.

We don't always know a dream's hidden meanings. For example, in the previous sample, both parties—the woman and her former husband—are still alive years later. So dreaming of death must not automatically be literally interpreted. In fact, literal interpretations are generally unhelpful.

After any emotional dream—holy or psychological—
lengthy pondering is often required. These dreams tend to
bypass linear, logical explanations. It could feel essential to
consult a spiritual helper, if, after a dream, we as dreamers are fraught with intense emotion. Also, our premature,
immature, or overly dramatic interpretations could be cues
that the helper's skill and experience can guide us. I suspect
I have drummed that point home.

Nevertheless, now I ask: in the case of the helper, what
does "qualified" mean to *you*? Most people want the other
to speak to and hear them at the level of awareness they
bring to the dialogue, to hear "where they're coming from"
instead of talking at, or over, their feelings or ideas.

If media polls can be believed, a lot of us detest jargon
and "psycho-babble." I'd guess the helper, as well, has lists of
desirable qualities for clients,

Many subtle variables are involved in a dialogue, which
in dream analysis might involve a professional association.
That is a relationship.

If a helper is tediously controlling, insists on this or that
interpretation, the dialogue may break down. As facilitators of such discussions, we are watchful for, say, our client's
shows of disinterest and other signals of either resistance
or *our* unproductive approach. Extensive training, skill,

and—yes—giftedness is required to further a dreamer's grasp of the words, symbols, and meanings of any dream. Facilitation of groups or individual sessions is sometimes more of an art than a science. (Which is why a trusted friend is frequently as helpful to such discussions as a high price professional. Not always.)

All that said, in most respects, we all have an *inborn* giftedness to something unique to the sort of person we are, probably to the sorts of dreams we have. Paying attention and receptivity to our inner life can help develop our interpretive skills in many areas. So can the Bible, and a good dictionary.

One Helper's Issue: "Did God *really* say that?"

A man sensed his dialogue with a professional helper was becoming a hindrance. His helper was over-questioning the authenticity of what he, the dreamer, believed God was saying in one dream. The dreamer noted, "Around the time of that dream I felt my helper had become a stumbling block. *Then* I had the following dream:"

> In the dream, I was praying in the Spirit, hearing from the Lord, and loving it. Still dreaming, I awoke and in the next scene told my spiritual director about it. He said, 'Are you sure it was the Lord?

You know satan often disguises himself…' and, still dreaming, I grow aware that the seeds of doubt have been successfully planted in my heart. Still dreaming, I now hear the Genesis 3:1 serpent whisper, 'Are you sure God said that?'

Later, I discussed this with my spiritual director—a good and Godly person who listened. I wanted to share what I'd learned, in sleep. We now use Scripture as our touchstone whenever there's a question about whose 'voice' I've heard. I use my intuition at all times.

That dream seems to reinforce Jung's notion of *preexisting*— might we say "eternal"—verities, motifs, directives in some dreams. The dreamer *knew intuitively* what was true for him. I believe that's the effect an archetype can have on us. A photograph, a painting, one word, a fragrance, a line of poetry or melody can stimulate deep resonance with something eternally pertinent to us. We may not know exactly what that is, but we know something in that element is for us, subjectively underpinning our very life.

The dreamer had heard the voice of the Good Shepherd and the voice of the stranger he would not follow. (John 10:1–18) This represents yet more of the true learning described all along. Doesn't it take time, receptivity, and experience for most of us to *ignore* the serpent's questions?

In addition to the contemplative prayer and practices already discussed, art, music, drama, sculpting and other meditative activities (e.g., fishing, gardening, sewing, singing, etc.) can help us unearth a dream's hidden gold if we're reflective as we engage in these things. Almost any hands-on pastime that leads the mind to thoughtful employment, be it with pottery, pastry-making, finger painting, or planting tulip bulbs, can lessen the resistance that deafen " ears that hear."

How can we be sure that we're not led astray by our own fancies and desires? Like Clint Eastwood remarked in one of his films, "If you want guarantees, buy a toaster." Neither the psyche nor the ways of God are formulaic. Which could be one reason (among many) that Scripture reminds us to work out our salvation "with fear and trembling." (Phil.2:12)

Understanding the things of God is no paint-by-numbers affair.

Getting Real: Authenticity

Time-honored resources can help us explore a spiritual dream: For example, meditation on God's word or keeping study notes in a dream log (along with other notes, quotes—even photos or art images, poetry clips). All that might richly augment a study of relevant parables and, possibly, the optional dialogue with a profession helper. Some bible study groups, particularly those that have met together for a long time, may be invaluable to further understanding of the holy, or spiritual, dream.

We spoke earlier of testing the spirits of a dream. Other basics can integrate comprehension and strengthen faith. Without soaring off into flights of vain imaginings over some dream, we can contemplatively study [48] our chosen and preferred heritage of faith. Here is where we may be happily surprised at the answers we find in such resources as…

- sacred Scripture,
- sacred traditions,
- sacred devotional doctrines and instructions.

Many saints, within our own faith-walk, could have recorded their dreams that reveal patterns or teachings similar to those in our own holy dream. The mind of the ordinary dreamer and the saint, are quite alike whenever God's touch is involved. [49]

Poised Hearing

We receive our "dream instructions" differently—in ways suitable for us as individuals— fitting for the kind of mind and propensities we have, the type of person we are. So how

---

48 For a short work on *Contemplative Study,* see our Monograph IV, available from The Center, only while supplies last.

49 In the Book of Acts, when Peter says he perceives that God is no respecter of persons, it surely seems as though, in the context of holiness, we are all potentially equal.

might each of us best take delivery of our sacred profundities? Our wisdom and intuitive preferences count. And so do our solid traditions. I, for one, dislike swinging wildly from one extreme viewpoint to another. At best, we'r being balanced in our interpretations.

On the one hand, Jesus called us out of rigidity and into wisdom: "If the light in us is darkness, how dreadful that darkness will be." On the other hand, he told us not to live in our heads, not to over-think things, to be like a child—not childish, but spontaneous—to take no thought for ourselves but to study the lilies of the field in their effortless, natural beauty. (See Mt. 6:23–30) Authenticity means effortlessly being the beauty of who we are.

Being the Kind of Person We Are

A professor of mine used to say, "No one can grow whole without truthfully disclosing themselves to at least one other person." A lifetime of "professional" listening has taught me that there are many ways to reveal ourselves to another. Verbal disclosures are not always necessary.

An intuitive "hearer" will sense nonverbal revelations, and in a dialogue *that* understanding is essential. Whether we're in a Bible study group or having a heart-to-heart talk with our best friend, if we're in a dialogue, we have to hear one another's heart, and gently, wisely, tactfully, skillfully speak our truths to their truths. We don't need to s*ay* everything aloud. "TMI" can be a problem, sometimes.[50]

Occasionally, the other can't hear our gentlest, most adroit remarks. A practiced facilitator will have spent hours and hours in training to gain just such skill.

Feelings are on the line in a dialogue, and as much as humanly possible in such settings, a facilitator's function seems that of interpreter and good steward. Like physicians, effective helpers strive to "do no damage;" they invite the other's receptivity to the voice of the Good Shepherd. God has created that hearing capacity. By and large, it is a hearing or seeing into the heart of the other in some balanced or steadying fashion. I've worked with superior facilitators who tend to be unusually poised in touchy situations. There are some among us who are just *born* to that "hearing" work.

In hopes of furthering skilled, professional dialogue on such topics, I propose that...

a)   the dream notes, notebook or journal, *private,* can enhance confidential exploration.
And that...

---

50 TMI is our current term for "too much information" which in any, particularly group, settings can prove unwise.

(b) the helper(s) probably won't be first to explain a dream or, say, a verse of Scripture in dictatorial fashion. Both parties in a true dialogue are active, give-and-take participants. (And, is it too much to ask that no one talk too much or interrupt too often?)

The demise of insight occurs in a big way (but is not limited to) in times when an "expert" or authority figure ... [51]

- stimulates anxiety, guilt, doubt, submission, etc. in the other,
- is largely pedantic or legalistic, while disguising that as "caring."

Should each of us develop our list of qualities we want in a spiritual helper? Sometimes, perhaps even the "gut reaction" is enough.

---

51 A number of books are cropping up, containing lists of dream symbols, metaphors, images, etc.—sort of inventories to help us decipher the meanings of our dreams. I, for one, am loathe to consult such volumes—helpful though they seem—until *after* consulting my deepest heart and wisdom about a dream. Few things enrich the soul more than contemplating a dream's message—its nuances, symbols, and scenes—and praying about it, When, suddenly or gradually, through union with the Holy Spirit, we discover—*receive* — our truths, trust in God is strengthened, for "...in Thy Light, we shall see light." (Ps. 36:9)

Marsha Sinetar

Scripture and Word-Study

The next dream sample illustrates how one receives deeper meaning from a memorable dream independently, primarily with word and Scripture study. For the contemplative mind, with this method, one discovery leads to another.

The individual in the next sample experienced a wholly new identity within the deeper aspects of a spiritual dream. The dream itself seemed to say that everything about the dreamer that God touched turned into God. (The analysis, so called, comes from adaptations of the dreamer's journal. Underlined are words that the dreamer felt significant.)

One Dreamer's Sample: "A Consuming Fire"

The Dreamer's Background

I'd been considering Isaiah's words—that 'the Lord will come with fire,...' (Is. 66:15) and that our God is 'like a consuming fire' (Deut. 4:14). One day, Meister Eckhart's idea came to mind: Our distinctiveness in God, therefore our spiritual formation, is like fire: Everything the fire touches turns into itself.

The next night I dreamt I was walking through someone's house—not mine. Near a pile of used clothing was a bright spark. It starts a small flame. No one else is around. No one sees it but me. So I call out to the household and phone the fire department. They arrive, try in vain to extinguish the blaze, but it spreads, so everyone leaves

90

the house (safely). However, the <u>house</u>—and all the old clothes—are consumed by the fire.

I wake up, not at all troubled as one might suppose. I'm relieved that the people are safe, if also quite puzzled about that used clothing.

In a flash, I recall Gal. 3:27: Christ is worn, like a garment: As we have been baptized into Christ, we put on Christ—we wear our living God, like clothes. And that garment, is of a spiritual, not material fabric, being '...without seam, woven from the top.' (John 19:23)

So then came an intensifying faith, maybe an abiding—I sense strength and well-being and power emerging from what I can only describe as a completely new identity in Christ. Nothing can put me back into those 'old clothes' – they're gone, burned up.

The Dreamer's Sample Word Study (Notes)

The dreamer's "log" indicates the subsequent word study included...

- <u>Clothes</u> – could mean a garment or outer garment; a mantle; anything put on like a covering, e.g., wedding garb. One source tells me "clothes," like the "heavenly city," are the spiritual covering we put on. Note to self: keep researching this.
- <u>Fire, flame, spark</u> – in this dream, fire symbolizes the Holy Spirit quickening my true self, burning away old, material coverings, overlays.
- <u>House</u> – a dwelling place; (note: Could 'house' also mean consciousness? Keep researching this,

especially as relates to House of God, the House of the Lord, and householders.)

- Household – inhabitants of a house -- in this case, not *of* the household of God, not kindred, since the people in my dream were strangers. If people in dreams are parts of ourselves, then these householders may be false, "stranger" aspects of myself, that the fie (God) ushers out of my house. Wow. (Note to self: If our dwelling place or house is, metaphorically, consciousness, could a 'householder' be a thought in consciousness? Is a *spirit* a thought?)

The Dreamer's Meditation Notes

The dream log includes the following:

After locating definitions of meaningful words and images, I contemplated these along with my relevant issues. I sometimes keep a journal, but don't engage in dialogue with other(s). Although if I did, that could happen anywhere along the line. The key for me was forgetting myself—getting out of my 'earthly tent' or creaturely state of mind and seeing things from God's viewpoint. God is my consuming fire and my dream still teaches me to cast off the truly useless overlays of earthly existence.

———

Ample Patience & Pondering

If the dreamer senses a word or symbol has particular significance, then a general help is that such terms or symbols can be explored for both Scriptural and everyday usage.[52] That happens first by taking time to meditate on our own unique meanings. Some words mean one thing in a dictionary, but quite another in *our* use.

Authenticity is woven into all dreams. Themes may be alike the world over, but symbols, words, colors and so on will differ. Children can show us the way. If we're half-way alert we notice our youngsters' true nature, recognize what they love. From birth, one flares up instantly. The least little thing sets her off. The other is placid. One solves math problems effortlessly, loves the shape and play of numbers. The next fears single digits. Your daughter is mesmerized by wheels and gears, spots esoteric codes in their workings; her brother talks to sparrows.

As helpers, we may look to the natural enchantments of the dreamer (whatever his or her age), contrasting their delights to some dream symbols. The presence or

---

52   One of my Bible dictionaries instructs readers that *words* in the parables should be defined literally, not spiritually. Whether to follow such rules, of course, each decides for him or herself. By contrast, every parable has multiple layers and is rarely understood by literal means. Hence the need for repeated hearing, thoughtful and private study, bible study, dialogue, etc. Some holy dreams, like parables, teach us continually, from multiple vantage points.

absence of real enjoyment is one approach to a beginning dialogue, not the only one. An opening conversation is not a mechanical interview. It's a getting-to-know-you time.

Then, too, understanding a dream is not like reading a sports playbook. Often, nothing profound happens during a dialogue session, so can we take time afterwards to mentally meander, to welcome hidden understandings as these arrive? Some of us "meditate" best on anything, dreams included, while making chili or watching *The Simpsons*.

Some stunning insights come only *after* we've let go of trying, after releasing the rope of our mind's tug-of-war that's straining to pull some revelation out of our depths. . As a friend always says, "Let, let, *let* things come."

Usually, except for parables, any significant word or symbol cries out—almost immediately—for a dreamer's in-depth study. For instance, animal symbols or food, drink and other natural elements quickly can ignite the need to know more about some facet of a dream. One dreamer noted that country roads, villages and highways had always held special significance. For another, it was some kind of unknowable game. A woman who loves to cook kept dreaming of a New York deli.

By investing an hour or two in contemplative study at the start—right after a spiritual dream—we may find ideas crop up over time; light-bulbs turn on when least expected .

What's Beautiful or True?

When and how might spiritual dreams confirm that a high, increasingly wholesome aesthetic is emerging? One clue to the formation of holiness is simple, sincere awe. The dreamer's wonder about life, a dream, a friendship, and moving beyond that to all of creation, however mundane, increases. The holy dream may magnify a kind of global reverence. What seemed ugly, dreary, ordinary yesterday is, today, shining with the light of God. To quote an unknown author, after the holy dream, sometimes "even the stones sparkle."

Poets, artists, photographers and others with an eye for transcendent beauty seem more likely to be comfortable with the chaos and novelty of a dream's images. Even in normal routines, they often worship "visually." Those with auditory gifts may worship through their hearing. So rarely do we get encouragement for that in church, while the psalmists regularly celebrated music, song, and the clapping of hands. (Musicians and composers are known to receive whole scores and portions of melodies during sleep.)

A young pianist said, "Music is everything to me. Playing the piano is a prayer. " [53] That deviation from ritualized verbal prayer may trouble the more traditional among us, but is standard for the truly creative.

Emily Dickinson's lines seem of that creed: While others keep the Sabbath in church, she writes, "I keep it by staying at home, with the birds for a choir and an orchard for a dome." And while others get to heaven eventually, the poet tells us, "I'm going all along."[54]

Each scripturally based revelation is a "grace"—a gift of spiritual intelligence that lets one incubate and develop intuition or discernment of the Holy Spirit's impartation.

Apart from God, no one but the dreamer can know what a dream means. We engage in dialogue to help coax along a well-reasoned, *spiritual* understanding—never trying to "settle" any issue too quickly.

Forcing premature closure of understanding always violates the interior life. Perhaps it "quenches" or thwarts the

---

53 The psalms are full of instruction on such issues: "Make a joyful noise unto the Lord." (Ps. 100, and Ps. 98) seems a case in point. If our heart is glad in the Lord, we are praying – or, perhaps we *are* the prayer.

54 Emily Dickinson, *Some Keep The Sabbath Going To Church,*(1955) The poem can be found, and I think also the phrase "sparkling stones," in Robert Kennedy's lovely *Zen Spirit, Christian Spirit* (New York: Continuum, 1996). John Ruusbroec's discussion of the sparkling stones was my first introduction to the phrase in connection with the topic of holiness. (See my last chapter's ideas and title.)

Holy Spirit. (See 1 Thes. 5:19) Our hasty attempt to tie up loose ends usually is obvious: We grow anxious with unknowns or become impatient with uncertainty. Or try to resolve ambiguity, fast. Which rarely works. Spiritual insights are much like infant's teeth: they appear when ready. To try to force these out is stupid and abusive. Let's not abort the birth of some delicate thought-thread that's on it's way from Heaven.

———

CHAPTER 8

As in Heaven, So in Earth

And the light shines in darkness, and
the darkness knoweth it not.
(JOHN 1:5)

THE HOLY DREAM could well bring a bit of Heaven to earth, through us. And again: it tends to be more sequential in its story line than not. In other dreams, we morph into weird roles and scenarios. The holy dream provides guidance, inspiration, and corrective content. It is a grace by and through which the soul is capacitated to choose Light—"as in heaven, so in earth." Thus the holy dream's message is universally applicable, meant to benefit a wide range of others.

Growth Steps

That said, the holy dream usually brings highly personal guidance: Unique to us—intended to strengthen us where we are weak. Perhaps we'll slowly outgrow our timidity, learn about our calling, receive warnings (like the dreamer who sensed her very soul was "thirsty"). Or get clarifications about a moral dilemma. Returning to our overarching theme: God's image of *Himself* is revealed to us, as the holiness related to us for our time, our place, and position in life. So, incrementally, we'll want to choose toward the simple goodness at our very ground of being. That, too, is authenticity.

Usually, our germ of adoration of God and our fascination with deeply spiritual issues intensifies. The mother's heart expands in love; the poet's ardor for the cadence and metaphor of language deepens.

Holiness is alive with us, a way of being real that flows from our living God—in dreams, I suspect that's from the Spirit igniting our spirit, in love. (Gal. 3:5) And that love restores our ability to see with the eyes of our heart. We'll note that such restoration is superbly *creative*—if only on the inside of us. Those progressing toward spiritual wholeness tend to display the talents, the same single eye (for example, sober, devoted focus, incubation of seminal ideas, and love of discovery) as happens with every gifted artist, inventor and creative contributor. Power from *within* enables our "without," since outer affairs tend to mirror the inner. Not necessarily in a linear mode. Sometimes, those who are all aflame to create do so continually, without support, encouragement and without material success. Consider those artists, inventors, song writers, perhaps in your own family or circle of friends, who have contributed so much to us—such as a Van Gogh or an Emily Dickinson—but, who in their lifetime, are unrewarded and unrecognized. Our time frames are usually not God's.

From the start of this narrative, from, say, the story of Joseph, Jacob, or Daniel, we have seen that some who encounter God's grace during sleep—saints, mystics, ordinary people and gifted contemplatives—have a special *mind* or talent *for receiving* the things of God. The reality is: most of us have the same aptitude but may need to develop our eyes to "see" and our ears to "hear." Thus, traditional spiritual practices—deep, self-forgetful prayer, meditation, ancient contemplative methods of many sorts—help cultivate that inborn, if dormant, ability. What opens our inner capacities?

Since my teens, I've been a great admirer of Abraham Maslow. Now I disagree with him in one critical area. If I understand correctly, Maslow believed that special drugs (like LSD) might open our spiritual eyes. (They might, but at what cost to our faith?) My chief concern is thiat Maslow seemed to construct his ideas along *human,* not spiritual, lines. I suppose, for him all "peak experiences" start and stop within the human skull.[55]

55 Abraham Maslow, *The Farther Reaches of Human Nature* (New York, NY. An Esalen Book/Viking Press, 1971), 389. See also, A. Maslow, *Religions, Values, and Peak-Experiences* (New York. Penguin Books, 1977).

For me, God, the Spirit, some say Mind, is omnipresent, beyond space and time, beyond the physical brain, transcending our body.

Maslow's framework is popular. Perhaps growing more so these days. I'd propose that that is a different worldview. My experience is that in the transcendent encounter, God, Spirit, or Divine Mind is the Light that fades out unreality or darkness. Love escorts the *spirit* of our mind "upward" (or inward) so that thought is stilled, escapes its captivity by the body. (To some, that is an altered state. Might not that be what happens in deep contemplative prayer, near-death or after death? (And, yes, maybe in the holy dream.)

I propose that orthodox contemplative disciplines (and also many other things, like the agape love, or a true vocation) can instill the powers of our highest reach of awareness wherein we're not just thinking *about* spiritual matters: we *are encountering* Heaven.

And more, in my direct experience these ancient practices routinely bolster faith, bring on an altered state, enhance creativity and can provide stress-relief. Not too shabby for practices that are thousands of years old.

The medieval Flemish mystic, John of Ruusbroec, thought that *three states* help one attend to the issues of holiness. In religious individuals, I view those states as evidence of high creativity. Namely, we are...

- In love with God, not precisely ourselves; self-empty-ing in unity with God, striving to overcome with virtue their sin, unbelief, limitations, resistances.
- Vibrantly interior persons, constantly thinking about and practicing the virtues (not always with even moderate success).,
- Continually "dying" to ourselves (our false self) and coming to the end of ourselves, in unity with God.[56]

The *striving itself*, the struggle for virtue or overcoming or love in God can trigger inordinate creative power and spiritual experiences. Not the experiences, but the union with God is the goal of those seeking holiness.

Why don't we, as a culture, hear more about the parallels between high creativity and religious becoming? The latter, for instance, suggests a living progression of *lavish interior richness.* We die small deaths *daily* so as to live larger, more abundantly in the presence of the Lord. Both holy dreams and everyday, wash-the-dishes life help us do that.

The executive who declines co-workers' invitations to celebrate corporate successes with wild partying could face rejection. Despite that, there could flow new found power within him or herself – even when , as a result of that decision, the workplace seems less hospitable than before. That's because

56 John Ruusbroec. (John Farin, Editor-in-Chief). *The Spiritual Espousals and Other Works* (Mahwah, NJ: Paulist Press, 1985).

the executive's loyalty has been transferred to a higher plane of existence. Which fuels added life, more abundant life, a fresh infusion of vitality for life from Above. Dreams, and holy ones all the more, can stimulate such small-death choices.

The soul progressing toward holiness uses everything—joy and sadness; ease and pain—to unfold her good, her true, her beautiful. As within, so without. Eventually, the outer life will mirror the inner.

In the light of holiness, Ruusbroec also reminds us, the interior and hidden rays of God's glory are so bright that even the stones sparkle.[57] Our own choices help or hinder ability to see that shine.

Previewing these lines, reading what I've written here, I imagine a reader admitting that he or she craves that lucidity, but says however, "My days and nights are so hectic, so distracted. I'm like Martha—preoccupied with too many chores; unhealthily sidetracked by a million self-imposed duties. How to overcome that?"

There's no limit to the types of overcoming one can strive toward, and dream about. The goal, however impossible, is to surmount all things—from fear, doubt, or self-crippling lifestyles to toxic relationships—so as to receive a new name, become a pillar in God's temple, and "... go out no more." (Rev. 3)

---

57 Ruusbroec, *op cit* 1991, 189.

One dreamer's guidance came from a dream that helped her deal competently with something she had feared. Before that dream, as a rule, she'd dreaded and had trouble prevailing over adversity.

After her dream, instead of avoiding difficulty, she grew more active, became willing to "take care of business."

The next passages excerpt that dreamer's journal and word-study notes.

Another Sample: "A Sweet Savor"[58]

The Dreamer's Background

Before my dream, I'd been considering the realities of the cross—Jesus Christ's death and resurrection—and the full freedom of actually living in the risen Christ. Is that life possible for humans? Is it possible for me? If it is, I wondered, what might that surrender and subsequent triumph require?

Two of my own 'cross' experiences related to health issues. These were still raw, still too tough to examine closely. That prompted a dream about such matters—especially the freedom of what someone called 'living from the heart, beyond reason.'[59]

---

58 Savor could mean taste or *euodia*: fragrance, as in 2 Cor. 2:15 or Eph.5:2, usually as a sweet smell received in heaven from an offering, such as tithes, "good works", or in the extreme, Jesus' sacrifice. Also, according to Scripture, even our sacrifice (i.e., offering) of prayer can be received in that fashion.

59 For our purposes, you'll find only a few words underlined that were consequential to the dreamer. In fact, in a log or journal of dream notes one might underline a whole slew of meaningful words. Some words and images come to mind later, after the fact.

In my dream, I am seated at a great celebration—perhaps some athletic event, in the midst of a happy, rejoicing crowd. I am holding a large, lush bouquet of long-stemmed, red <u>roses</u>—apparently a <u>gift</u>. The <u>fragrance</u> rises up to me, but I have work to do: my job is to cut off every <u>thorn</u>. I sense that my task is a pre-condition to partaking either of the sweet savor of the <u>flowers</u> or the celebration.

I work with <u>detachment</u>, watching myself <u>handle</u> the thorns carefully. It seemed a lucid dream. Before, I'd felt poorly; after, I was energized, lighter about my current discouragement, feeling that I am well. Today, many months later, I still have faith that I'll be healthy and productive into advanced age. Something changed.

Review: The Economy of Grace

1. The dreamer above prayed for interpretive guidance. The note indicates...

    Pain and suffering can mean many things. In the context of my life at this time, cutting thorns, for me, signifies a surrender to my faith, not to fear. And removing hardship by handling it, by growing in trust from that.

    I see that by facing my thorns, or fears, I can be a more reliable, trustworthy comfort to others who suffer, and through Christ, can overcome things in some subtle— if not always overt—way.

2. To grapple with lasting impressions, the dreamer kept notes, writing in the log...

    One can 'cast the burden' or 'offer up' one's suffering. I sense right now my task is to recover what one bible dictionary calls "the economy of grace"—cut off dead laws in favor of the living Truth. The dismal "laws" of the medical establishment was a thorn that, for me – I don't say for everyone!- needed to go. I've replaced the medical model with a Christly model.

'Cutting' thorns has come to mean, using St. Paul's analogy, circumcising old ways; wherein the flesh no longer dictates life's show. A new, better covenant is my condition for success and God's favor.[60] For the sweet fragrance of God's holiness, I'm learning to eliminate a slavish response to 'the law,' false guilt, or despair. It's slow going, a lifetime's work.

3. The dreamer studied words and symbols related to the dream:

Over time, my word study revealed that thorns can 'symbolize evil in the heart that chokes the Word.' Or be 'a sign of desolation.' I try to handle these miseries, one by one—some quickly, some grudgingly, slowly—in order to live in, not merely talk about, life in the risen Christ. My dream was meaty in its significance; everyone receives trials in ways that can strengthen faith and transform life forever. (James 1:12; Heb. 2)

4. The dreamer entered into a dialogue with a spiritual friend about the dream's enduring message(s).

However, what a dialogue—or journal work, etc.—could make known over much time, the unction of the Holy Spirit can reveal in an instant. Which may explain why contemplative prayer is so helpful in these matters.

---

60 W. E. Vines, et al., *Vines Complete Expository Dictionary of Old and New Testament Words* (Nashville, TN: *Thomas* Nelson, 1984), 102.

Some call that revealing prayer *praying in the Spirit.* To others, that last phrase means "self-vanishing." A friend describes it as, "Going out of self, into God." Whatever our words, in these moments we leave self-involvements for "God-involvement."[61]

As for the dreamer above, an expanded, universal aesthetic seemed to develop, that included...

a. a new sense of beauty—even an occasional rejoicing in trials— where before certain challenges seemed too painful to bear,

b. an energizing hope, where before there had been hopelessness,

c. a restored sense of being a "sweet savor" to God.

That dreamer also noted,

I'm not called to martyrdom, but to prayer. Contemplation and ongoing study have shown me that by focusing on Reality—God and how God has created things to be—sometimes now I can, in an inexplicable way, experience all things as an incomprehensible echo of that word to 'consider it all joy.'[62]

------

61 For a lengthy discussion of mystical union in everyday life, see M. Sinetar, *Ordinary People as Monks & Mystics* (Mahwah, NJ., Paulist Press, Revised, w/Preface. 2007).
62 James 1:2.

CHAPTER 9

When Stones Sparkle

And the gates of it shall not be shut at all by day for
there shall be no night there.
(Revelation 21:25)

YES, THERE IS a certain altitude of consciousness—a state of grace and union with God, one supposes—where stones can sparkle. And, certainly, that perspective can, as with St. Paul (when he was still Saul) arrive suddenly—through no good of our own. That state is also a gradual, enduring, growth of awareness. Soon comes the conscious choice to turn our very soul upward to the Light that is our Life. (John1:4) That turn is our choice. I see it first as a perceptual state, ultimately as an aspect of holiness, wherein our "Mary" and our "Martha" (i.e., our inactive and active sides), become harmonious siblings, integrated so that quarrelling traits and inconsistencies smooth out, cooperate, finally make sense in the larger scheme of things.

It's strange to think of holiness as a choice. Two summary questions, and one is rhetorical: Isn't reaching out for holiness life's *most creative* choice? Don't the saints and saintly sorts whom you admire most make that choice? The enthusiasm of anyone who advances in that way is obvious. That may explain, as a previous dreamer realized, why the Bible tells us to "Consider it all joy." (James 1:2) And why one of the fruits of the Spirit *is* joy. Joy is present-centered, creative, independent of things, and a natural—effortless—state. Happiness is situational; joy is of God.

Just so: we have seen that some dreams, holy I've called them, infuse the dreamer with cheer.

Not only dreams, but uncomplicated rest also can result in gladness, revived energy, new ideas. We've probably noticed that we muse about our highest potentials during our easiest, most relaxing times—while napping, fly-fishing, watching the moon and the stars. Or marveling at our baby playing with her toes. We'll listen to Handel's *Messiah*, or sit meditatively in the midst of stimulating others—say, at a lecture—and, spontaneously, our heart sings, our mind soars to celestial realms. Abruptly in thought we spot unexpected prospects that solve all kinds of family or work problems. Some of us even write down these nuggets, worthless though they may turn out to be. One never can tell.

Painters, composers, sculptors, writers, scientists, parents and all types of leaders report awakening from seemingly dreamless nights with a sense of well-being. Either the weight of a major concern has lifted, or some much-needed confidence returns. A friend, battling a knotty relocation issue, phoned to say, "Last night I dreamt I was settled and happily so. I sense things will fall into a good place."

One Sunday morning, your author woke up with the present narrative—i.e., this book—full blown in mind. While sipping coffee, the entire outline got sketched out. By Monday morning, I'd keyed the early text into the computer. By Wednesday, the title and sections were set. Three days later, I'd completed the entire first draft. (A poet friend, having experienced the same thing, said, "It's somewhat passive, as if my verse was written *for* me.")

While light-bulbs go on as we sleep, fine tuning such ideas can take years. Never mind delays. The blessing has been cast; the "seed" of the completed thing has fallen—joyfully—into our ground of being, planted *in mind* during, and after, a good rest. Sometimes these prompts lead nowhere. The choice to follow, or ignore, such leadings is entirely *ours.*[63] Choice, and I may say this again later, is always service of some sort.

---

63 In fact, nearly every book, title of books, and text modifications to books, recordings, and even business letters have come either while I'm asleep, just waking up, or just falling asleep (in what is known as a *hypnogogic* time, or image-rich reverie). Or, while looking the other way as it were—watching films, listening to music, driving, weeding, etc. I cannot stress strongly enough the need for rest , incubation, and renewal in the creative process.

When Is Sleep Creative?

Who doesn't wake up occasionally with snippets (or wide vistas) of some business vision or personal goal, at hand—with completed pictures in mind of an undertaking we didn't even know we'd had? That alone tells us our sleep has been productive. No wonder many creative types sleep with pen and paper by their bedside. Once fully awake, too frequently like wisps of smoke these good ideas vanish, and we can't retrieve them.

Oddly enough, and this is merely another personal digression, I have had some of my *most* creative dreams when exhausted, and as emphasized throughout these pages, when fascinated by any idea. Strength of absorption seems a prod to vivid stories, solutions and, yes, that "transcendent" or creative sleep we've discussed.[64]

Stravinsky, while working on another composition, *received* the germ of his vision for his *Le Sacre du Printemps*. One night, he dreamt the entire scene of symbolic, ritual dances which, still later, he sketched out and featured in that symphony. Composition, invention, any application of the imagination (as in healing prayer, the strengthening of faith, etc.) seems born of rarified thought

---

64 In my early career, working with intense and innovative corporate leaders, I attempted to write of a state of mind—contemplative, image-laden, solution-oriented—in *Developing a 21st-Century Mind*. The people who took to it were psychologists and psychiatrist; not so much for the mass market reader who received that work as too mystical and esoteric. Alas.

processes—the higher reaches of our spiritual faculties where disbelief is suspended or beliefs shaped, improved, renewed, and all vain imaginings cast down. One often wonders: Is *every* dream insight a grace of the Holy Spirit?

A Few Traits of Creative Giftedness

During sleep, our flashes of brilliance and every holy dream (by which I mean every emanation resulting from the soul's reverential turn to God) is of God. Over the years, I've learned that the messages of holy dreams work within us— *long* after sleep—for the soul's good, her true, her beautiful. Others think differently.

The choice to grow toward holiness is a *response* to a call, an all-out creative leap. Choice is a "Yes" or "No" answer. It seems accompanied by the conscious choosing and arranging to walk in our truths. Which can be risky business.

The "Yes" choosers (i.e., those who affirm the call to holiness) are seized by a sigh of possibility. Or, as creativity research tells us about innovative types, they tend to be caught up by an embryonic vision, summons, or noble intent. Here again we may find similarities between highly religious (or spiritual) and highly creative minds. The ballet dancer and the contemplative will, at some point of oneness with their work (be it dance or worship) feel "In this act, in this moment, I am one with my dance; I am one with my prayer." Both dancer and worshiper could feel, "My whole being is praying, I am being prayed, I *am* prayer."

Those talented monks, mystics, and saintly sorts who reach out (or feel predestined) for holiness share attributes with other talented *creative* minds in other walks: intense focus, single-mindedness, a beyond-"self" sense of destiny. (One sometimes even hears the religious drive called *God-intoxication*.)

The creatively gifted in secular and religious fields both require huge amounts of uninterrupted thinking-time—which includes non-doing. And solitude.

Here I do not mean emotional isolation, but that lovely aloneness that lets us enjoy our own thoughts.

Wasn't it English novelist and philosopher Aldous Huxley who suggested that the more elevated and powerful a mind, the more it would incline itself to the religion of solitude.

Our Need for Rest & Renewal

Bursts of illumination—such as talented musicians or novelists experience—*require* rotations of activity and restoration. Passionate, constant thought on any theme transforms the thinker—particularly *if* that fidelity of mind "breathes," rests, gets refreshed.[65]

For one thing, steady concentration on a matter can be exhausting. For another, to me that explains why the highly gifted partake of naps, musing, watching television, travel, sailing; all such times invite day-dreaming – a propensity that seems a healthy habit. We scold our children for day-dreaming in school. We fault our politicians and business people for too much time spent on the golf course. *But:* In that rest there is renewal: time to incubate (consciously or not) their solutions, their pet themes.[66] Or get much needed time out from these.

Incubation waters the seed of creative thought. Which is one reason not to entertain guilt-feelings for taking Sunday naps. And probably is why our grandparents taught us to "count our blessings" before sleep. It's wise to sleep in a climate of gratitude.

My creative friends (and I, too) prefer to, and perhaps quite naturally, think *into* an incubating sort of mind while falling asleep. The reason? It's like hatching an egg. There's a subjective warmth in such reveries that nurtures the birth of ideas.

---

65 An innovative business friend intentionally travels alone for some of his best ideas; he also has engaged in "extreme sports", the mind-set of which he says frees him from everything *except* the here-and-now. And that seems to clear the way for fresh insights.

66 Marsha Sinetar, *Developing a 21st-Century Mind* (New York: Random House, 1990).

There is also an organizing function of mind before and during creative acts. Sleep, catnaps, recharging inner batteries help that job. We know, for example, that the gifted scientist *and* the gifted leader *and*, I submit, the gifted religious strive for years (and quite capably, too, one observes) to fulfill their goals. Where many of us grow weary and quit chipping away at our sense of the possible, these individuals endure decades, maybe a lifetime, of unknowns, ambiguity, hostility. Perhaps their capacity to draw out the strength to persevere comes from within, in part from the love they have for what they do. That love stimulates a kind of buoyancy, resilience, a willingness to get up and try again.

Author Lionel Tiger asks what is it in the creative, in the athlete, (and the great ones all the more) that makes them keep going when their minds and bodies cry out for them to stop? He wonders what it is in the young dancers that crowd in and out of a dance studio near his home, that makes them exert their will and their bodies until they can't anymore? Whatever it is, he concludes, it isn't pessimism.[67]

I believe Love is the X-factor.

Then, too, as I'm suggesting, such endurance comes from possessing, and tapping into, the opulence of our inner life. Which as noted seems enriched by continuous habits of absorption, incubation of "seed" ideas, and renewal.

---

67 Lionel Tiger, *Optimism* (New York: Simon and Schuster. 1979), 256-257.

Surely, the latter integrates all sorts of components of mental functioning, including shaping, arranging, and *composing* of projects, or a whole life to which one is ideally suited. In that last function, it's as if each life is a symphony with many moods, parts, movements.

Scholar and author, Professor Vera John-Steiner addresses the need for what she terms *cycles of rest and activity*. She helps us appreciate the complex skills involved in shaping the life – or art – we want. She writes, "Composition thus emerges as a *process* which demands, as do other creative endeavors, an ability to synthesize germinal ideas with elaborate structures."[68] (Those "structures" are ideational, not necessarily material.)

Would we better serve our lives by considering it as a long term, creative composition? If you ask what this has to do with the holy dream, I'd answer that even a short nap can refresh the mind – yes, and perhaps bring us a dream-fragment that serves our ability to creatively structure the day, the week, the business report, the sermon. Little arrangements add up to lovely compositions and life itself.

Those of us with strong creative drives need healthy sums of rest, but often work against ourselves by laboring endlessly. Some of us cannot stop working.

---

68 Vera John-Steiner, *Notebooks of the Mind* (Albuquerque, NM: University of New Mexico Press, 1985), 153, 155, 156.

Do we try to sustain an unvarying forward movement as if we were machines? If, to function properly, even computers need to be turned off and restarted now and then, how much more do we – spiritual beings – need to "turn off." Unless renewal lubricates the wheels of our mind, *creative* thought can rust and malfunction. Once again, I for one spot similarities between inventive and religious, particularly contemplative, minds.

Contemplatives, like other creatives, usually seek solitude, silence, and spells of seeming inertness. There is a difference between idleness and the passivity rooted in contemplation. A spiritual director might help us understand that difference as it relates to our own life.

Generally, creative or contemplative indolence, whatever the Puritans believed, draws thought into the here-and-now. Or, into far off and future potentials. What some corporate planners and strategists call "blue sky" meetings, where ideas flow freely, in my experience can be replicated by an afternoon spent snoozing on the couch, or listening to Bach's *Cello Suites.* The harmonious operations of the mind's faculties are in play when one has found fulfillment in what Scripture calls the *rest* (*anapausis*) of God. That is a rest *in* work, not rest from work.[69]

For creative minds, that work is deceptive: activity is continually going on *inwardly*, while outwardly one could appear

---

69   Vines, *op cit* 959

inert. Engagement draws the creative mind inward. Which also happens in dreams. That is what it means to be occupied.

That creative rest is a necessity for those we are discussing.[70]

We should hear much more about that. Most executives – and also the clergy, physicians, health care professionals, caretakers of the ill, young seminarians, new parents, and so many others – usually work under a constant, crushing weight of duties. Industry leaders frequently pride themselves on their ability to arrive at work early, stay late, keep doing things better, faster, cheaper. Younger, junior executives emulate that pace.

Professor and author John Briggs details the seeming lethargy and rest needed by highly creative people. Many gifted types endure a life of seeming paradox: They might criticize themselves for the very "sulphuric laziness" that their absorption with projects demands.[71]

In fact, fretful, ultra-ambitious, strife-filled routines block that creative rest. (See Hebrews 3:10-11)

We are not robots. If we experience burnout, it could mean we've neglected restorative practices. Which, for contemplatives, is the kiss of death to what Jesus called partaking of "the good part, that shall not be taken away." (Luke 11:42)

---

70 So few of us understand this issue, it might be helpful to share the chapter with interested others. (Then again, maybe not.)

71 John Briggs, *Fire in the Crucible* (Los Angeles: J. Tarcher, 1990), 200–215.

The Mystical Mind—Endangered Species?

Now consider the contemplative (aka mystical) mind: Engaged, enraptured and typically inventive. That last quality could partly be due to the fact that , at least for those in secular settings, there is no road-map or mental model for shaping their life. Usually, there's no one in their sphere to show the way or encourage. Quite the reverse. The culture works against it.

A parent, secretary, or truck driver with a heart for prayer tends to swim upstream of family plans when looking for moments and places at home to worship in solitude. Said one person, "I see signs of contempt on the face of my spouse when I want to spend the morning alone in order to pray and read Scripture." Such people may ask, "Can the spiritual dream help me converse with friends who are bored silly by my religious talk?"

For such conflicts, Oswald Chambers is stern: God shows us the light and asks us to accept it, and walk in it. *He* will put things right. The holy dream can infuse us with boldness to consider Chambers' tough love stance.

Speaking personally, not until I was forty or more years old did anyone encourage my contemplative nature. Nor did any close family or lifelong friends know (or want to know) anything about contemplative life.[72] How many parents really understand the needs of their creative and/or religiously inclined children? As a former school principal, before that a teacher of the Gifted and Talented programs, I'd say very few. Whatever the talents, a gifted child can make parents uneasy.[73]

Creativity scholars tell us that inventive people, including young children, tend to be caught up by—wholly enraptured with— a *seed* of sturdy, stubborn ambition. That seed presses for growth all their lives.

With the religious, the seed of ambition is no less sturdy or stubborn than it is with an Edison or an Einstein. For the religious, the goal is God: union with the Divine; all-out Oneness.[74]

The seed is "within itself," we read in Gen. 1:11: So in this case, it appears our very *life* can unfold from renewal's germination. In *all* highly motivated people there's a fire in the belly to capture some great goal. Not only activity, but also rest seems critical to its attainment.

---

72 I believe I spoke about that in *Elegant Choices, Healing Choices* (Mahwah, NJ., Paulist Press. 1988).

73 See, for e.g., Alice Miler, *Drama of the Gifted Child* (New York, Basic Books., 1997). And my own *Spiritual Intelligence.*

74 See: Psalm 27:4, What, I ask you, is the difference of intensity of focus between the Psalmist's quest "to dwell in the House of the Lord forever" (some texts say "... all the days of my life") and a college youngster seized by the desire to invent some next generation computer? I am *not* comparing the value of these two goals. Just the inner life: Each sort draws on a fountain of passion – love – from *interior* resources.

I propose those monks, mystics, and contemplatives who aim at holiness (or what Underhill refers to as "the unitive life") could display comparable attributes of mind to those in the creative arts, science and the like. For the most part, they are as absorbed, single-minded, self-governing as a Bach, a Monet, a Mel Brooks, a Stevie Wonder.

Everyone who pursues a robust ambition is not creative or even talented. However, in drawing parallels between these gifted contributors, it helps to look at best cases. Whatever our walk or work in life, by our striving for excellence, we can tone up society, the community in which we live.[75]

Consider a few creativity traits of contemplatives who tend to be …

- more focused on God than "self,"
- more engaged with themes of goodness, truth, beauty, virtue, and justice or mercy than with issues of sociability or commerce,
- more able than most (indeed eager) to spend time alone with the beloved object of their contemplation,
- more open than closed to experiences of inner life, novelty, the chaos of the unknown, feelings, etc.,[76]

75 The best discussion of that idea I find in John W. Gardner, *Excellence* (Harper Row. New York. 1965).

76 Evelyn Underhill, that great scholar of universal mysticism called this "the inward odyssey." Like moths to the flame, mystics, contemplatives are drawn to an apprehended primal Reality, or Person, or sensed Divine Love.

- more transcultural than not (i.e., accepting of universal ideas, truths).

With such minds, *the interior gaze* is preoccupied, fertile, especially if one is rooted and grounded in that one true Light that is Life.

Such as these may well infuse some degree of Heaven into earth.

Holiness: The Focus on Light

We are still speaking of the *dream*s of those who are spiritually minded, perhaps particularly the converted, "twice-born" or "born again." Which, as noted earlier, I do *not* equate with religiosity, denominationalism or church membership. Nor am I meaning a private, elitist faith. I mean uninterrupted intimacy of *the Divine relationship.*

Holiness involves our turn to God. That principle relates to previous notions of earthly holiness: we saw earlier with athletes, dancers, and others who possess an enviable endurance, resilience, and optimism, to be motivated by Love is just practical. The more love we have, the more we lift our mind to the Spirit, the better. (See Rom. 8:6)

To illustrate: It is said that St. Catherine of Genoa was "never without the consciousness of her tender Love." Nor did she ever fail in her practical duties because of her Godly awareness.

Then, too, she often side-stepped admission of sin—not because she believed she was perfect, but because her radical love of God had a kind of John 15 constant "abiding."

Dreams can reflect that posture, wherein we who are "from below" (i.e., we mere mortals) begin to view others and things "from above"—from the Lord's perspective, as a result of a spiritual dream. Even with that elevated influence, it's natural to swing back and forth, to move between our old way and the new. Devotion, for instance, is not constant, virtuous, positive momentum. Abraham, David, the apostles, despite extraordinary intimacy with God, were full of flaws. Moses, in his younger days, killed a man.

By twenty, Teresa of Avila—one of our most famous saints—had "established a pattern" of intense religious ardor and "backsliding" to worldliness.[77] So we, too, who are mostly bumbling backsliders, can relax. It's likely we'll seesaw between healthy and unhealthy growth. Dreams of all sorts are a real-world support in such growth, as pointed out in the Preview. It may have been Maslow who noticed that *healthy* growth involves wholesome advances as well as regressions, taking time out, stepping back, retreating to lick our wounds. So let's forgive ourselves and others for occasional retreating to safer fields.

Doesn't that forgiving posture about our own and others' backsliding require empathy of a Christly order, and a

---

77 Donald Weinstein and Rudolph M. Bell, *Saints and Society* (Chicago: University of Chicago Press, 1982), 41.

creative bent? Here is one area, among many, that shows us other links between creativity and the holy dream. We can awaken from a dream with a change of heart – for the better. (As did the widow who realized she had forgiven her husband, and loved him "forever".) The holy dream draws our imagination into such profound and poignant scenarios that we "see" deeper truths than we can in our waking hours.

Studies suggest that the more creative we are the more we tend to dream vividly, and recall our dreams. Further, with heightened creativity as well as spiritual wholeness we gain a sort of rarified aesthetic, an ability to appreciate nuance and delicacy in all things, including people.

My mother had that "rarified aesthetic." She lacked formal schooling, or training as an artist, yet knew without being told by pundits, pollsters, or magazine reviewers what was fine art and superb operatic or theatrical performance. She also knew instantly what was low. With her unerring ear and eye for duplicity, phoniness, and the vulgar, she immediately spotted whatever was coarse, and what was refined. Her taste was sublime.

Then, too, both she and my paternal grandmother had exquisite empathy. It sometimes actually hurt to notice the intricacies of feeling in others that they noticed: mood, pain, vulnerability. No doubt, their empathy hurt them more since the agape kind of love is tough to bear.

Kermit the Frog said it another way, "It's not easy being green."

Easy or not, is it even possible to overlook the flawed stuff of our world without a skillful, practiced *spiritual* imagination? Or a degree of good, perhaps quirky, humor? Or mercy and unfeigned compassion? And don't those qualities reflect a vibrant inner life? By which I mean high spiritual intelligence—intuition, wisdom, discernment of everyday, warts-and-all beauty? That's the inner eye that sees "eternity in a grain of sand," as William Blake wrote. That sight flows from the divine love.

One has only to witness a parent's sacrificial love for his or her child to marvel at that unadulterated ardor. Can the holy dream further such love? You bet. And that's what most of us want.

The Hearing Ear "Hears" Holiness

In the context of my educator's role—decades that required a trusted listener— I've been honored to learn from and work with so many different ages and types of people: from first graders through doctoral students and executives and the elderly in life-care communities; from parents of students to health-care professionals and CEOs of multinational corporations.

I heard adults trying their utmost to do their best for those who depended on them, and children trying to be good, to do good, and to make their parents proud.

Variously, I listened to the secret aspirations and the dreams that, to me, represented the quest for wholeness we're exploring. Young and old *knew* they wanted uncomplicated goodness. Such a simple goal. And yet seemingly so complicated to attain.

The philosopher, Soren Kierkegaard called that the Good that, *in all its forms* and expressions, is the *One* same Good. Then, too, in his *Confession,* Tolstoy, the great Russian writer (e.g., *War and Peace)* admits that from early childhood all he ever wanted was just to be good. Only in maturity, after having traveled far from that goal, through fame and other worldly distractions, did he choose to turn back and reconsider his youthful ambition of goodness.

Repeatedly, I heard and still hear that yearning in people who ask, "What do you think that dream means? It feels like I'm being prodded to something good, it feels important. I keep thinking about it...."

Such questions reflect our shared yearning for God's eternal Good with all its fruit. I imagine almost every reader has heard the same hope expressed by someone much loved.

If we're alert to such things we'll sense that wish nonverbally, most easily from our children. They'll shyly confide in us, possibly after doing something wrong, whispering a soft, "I'm sorry," along with a desire or promise to be good.

Do we hear what's really being said? If so, we have "ears to hear" the wish for spiritual wholeness. And can encourage self-and-other to seek the Way of holiness. (Is. 35:8)

It's said that the Holy Spirit opens up the Bible for us, illuminates a word, a line, or verse, teaching us what we need to know. Which includes the holy dream. In sum, these dreams transmit our spiritual good: Guiding us as the dreamer into blessed possibilities; prompting us to be so daring as to strive for that Good which, however we might express it, is one and the same Good in all its forms.

———

Aren't we all – not just the saints and saintly, but all we ordinary sorts – at least occasionally, meant to dream the dreams that, by grace, move the soul beyond her dry and dusty season into the transcendent sleep that is so sweet?

Awake or asleep, the holy dream informs the soul of things she longs to know. These dreams sometimes are frightening; sometimes they soothe. Yet holy dreams draw the soul closer to her God. Here comes the "juice" we really want: power from on high, sheer goodness, wisdom, *inner wealth*. That's not power as the world knows it, not power as a materialist's heart craves it. It's that 'spark of the soul" as the ancients said of many things, the igniting that lets the soul run the race for which she was born.

At first, such generating power is *perceptual*—a capacity to see the very stones sparkle. Surely, that fuels ability to discern the unction and play of the Holy Spirit, with us *always*—even at night, even in sleep, even in dreams.

Such power is like soft rain falling on our thirsty ground of being; living water, transforming us from barren into "good ground," finally fruitful, meaning *karpos* – "...the visible expression of power working *inwardly*."[78]

———

> For ground that drinks the rain which often falls upon
> it, and brings forth vegetation useful for those for whose
> sake it is also tilled, receives a blessing from God.
>
> (HEBREWS 6:7)[79]

---

78 Vines, *op cit* 463. (Italics mine for emphasis.)
79 New American Standard Bible.

Author's Thank You

Three people helped me so much in the production of this book.

Patricia A. Davis, Jon M. Sweeney, and Roberta L. LaVorne were invaluable during the word processing, editing and proofreading of countless versions. I am grateful. Any errors are my own.

About the Author

Prolific author and pioneering educator, Marsha Sinetar, has devoted the last 40 years to the study and theme of spiritual wholeness, "our *true* learning."

Having worked with all ages and types of people – primary grade through college and doctoral students; Fortune 500 leaders through elder-care professionals; public and private sector constituents — Sinetar considers the quest for spiritual wholeness our universal wish and "our life's most creative, critical choice." In her corporate capacity, Sinetar advised some of America's most gifted minds. She sees us all, young and old alike, longing for simple goodness, hoping to *discover how to be, and how to live, the truth and beauty of who we are created to be.*

Her still growing body of work closes the seeming gap between our material and spiritual life. Whereas her earlier, twenty or more, books speak to a wide popular audience, her current ideas flow from the direct, prayerful dictates and experience of her Christian contemplative life.

Her newest ideas may appeal most to those of us with the heart and spiritual maturity to bear the Love, the Beauty and the subtle nuances of "the Light that is our Life." Sinetar's hallmark approach is researching and establishing productive mental models for learning. She lives and works "as quietly and simply as possible" in the Pacific Northwest.[80]

---

80 If you enjoyed this book and/or are a helping professional (e.g., clergy, counselor, spiritual director, etc.) seeking to extend your leadership reach in these themes, please visit www.marshasinetar.com

131

Dreams unto Holiness

_____

_____

_____

_____

_____

_____

_____

_____

_____

_____

_____

_____

_____

_____

_____

_____

_____

_____

_____

_____

_____

_____

_____

_____

_____

Marsha Sinetar

Printed in Great Britain
by Amazon